The Methuen Drama Modern Play
forefront of modern playwriting and
developmens in modern drama sin
fiftieth anniversary of Methuen Dra
2009 as Methuen Drama Modern
readers a ch ction of the best

Oh V   ›vely War

Oh What a Lovely War was first performed at the Theatre Royal, Stratford
East, London on 19 March 1963. The scheme for a chronicle of the First
World War, told through the songs and documents of the period, was
given flesh and blood in Joan Littlewood's Theatre Workshop, where
every production, and this one *par excellence,* was the fruit of close co-
operation between writer, actor and director. The whole team partici-
pated in detailed research into the period and in the creative task of
bringing their material to life in theatrical tenus.

The result was an entertainment which won the acclaim of London
audiences and critics and the *Grand Prix* of the *Théâtre des Nations* festival in
Paris in 1963 and has become a classic of the modem theatre. In 1969 the
film version became a popular success in its own right.

Joan Littlewood's Theatre Workshop company was set up at the end
of the war and started by touring in Wales, the industrial north and
Scotland. In 1953 they moved into the Theatre Royal, Stratford,
London E15 and remained there for the next eleven years during which
time they built up an international reputation. Their best work included
classical revivals like *Volpone* and *Edward II* and new plays like The *Quare
Fellow* and *The Hostage* by Brendan Behan, *A Task of Honey* by Shelagh
Delaney and musical plays like *Fings Ain't Wot* They *Used T' Be* by Frank
Norman and Lionel Bart.

Joan Littlewood's Musical Entertainment

Oh What a Lovely War

BY

Theatre Workshop
Charles Chilton, Gerry Raffles
and Members of the Original Cast

Title suggested by
TED ALLEN

Military adviser
RAYMOND FLETCHER

Revised and restored to the original version by
Joan Littlewood

B L O O M S B U R Y
LONDON • NEW DELHI • NEW YORK • SYDNEY

Bloomsbury Methuen Drama
An imprint of Bloomsbury Publishing Plc

50 Bedford Square
London
WC1B 3DP
UK

1385 Broadway
New York
NY 10018
USA

www.bloomsbury.com

Bloomsbury is a registered trade mark of Bloomsbury Publishing Plc

First published 1967
Reprinted by Bloomsbury Methuen Drama 2006, 2008, 2011, 2012, 2013 (twice)

This edition published in 2014
© Joan Littlewood Production Ltd 1965, 2000, 2014

All rights whatsoever in this play are strictly reserved and application for performance etc.
should be made before rehearsals by professionals to The Sayle Literary Agency,
1 Petersfield, Cambridge, CB1 IBB and by amateurs to Samuel French Ltd, 52 Fitzroy Street,
London W1P 6JR. For USA and Canada, all enquiries should be addressed to Amy E. Love,
Wedgewood Productions, P.O. Box 440, Crownsville, MD 21032; and/or 600 Cornelius
Point Road, Stevensville, MD 21666, USA. No performance may be given unless a licence
has been obtained.

Note to the Reader
This is playscript and should be read as such.

No rights in incidental music or songs contained in the work are hereby granted and
performance rights for any performance/presentation whatsoever must be obtained from the
respective copyright owners.

British Library Cataloguing-in-Publication Data
A catalogue record for this book is available from the British Library.

ISBN: PB: 978-1-4725-8464-9

Library of Congress Cataloging-in-Publication Data
A catalog record for this book is available from the Library of Congress.

Typeset by Deanta Global Publishing Services, Chennai, India
Printed and bound in Great Britain

Acknowledgements

Lines from the songs, 'Belgium put the Kibosh on the Kaiser', 'Hold Your Hand Out, Naughty Boy', 'I'll Make a Man of You', 'Goodbye-ee', 'Sister Susie's Sewing Shirts', 'Pack Up Your Troubles', 'Row, Row, Row,', and 'Hitchy-Koo' are reprinted by permission of the copyright owners and publishers, Francis Day & Hunter Ltd; the copyright owners in Australasia ('Belgium put the Kibosh on the Kaiser', 'Hold Your Hand Out, Naughty Boy', 'I'll Make a Man of You', 'Goodbye-ee', 'Sister Susie's Sewing Shirts', 'Pack Up Your Troubles'), Messrs. J. Albert & Son Pty. Ltd; the copyright owners in Canada ('Pack Up Your Troubles'), Chappell & Co. Inc., New York; the copyright owners in Canada and Australasia ('Row, Row, Row,'), H. von Tilzer Music Publishing Co; and the copyright owners in Canada and Australasia ('Hitchy-Koo,'), La Salle Music Publishers, Inc. 'Keep the Home Fires Burning': copyright © 1915 by Ascherberg, Hopwood & Crew Ltd; copyright renewed; reprinted by permission of Ascherberg, Hopwood & Crew Ltd, London, and Chappell & Co. Inc., New York. 'I Wore a Tunic' is a soldiers' parody of the song 'I wore a Tulip', published by Ascherberg, Hopwood & Crew Ltd, London and Leo Feist Inc., New York. Lines from the song, 'Are We Downhearted' are reproduced by permission of Lawrence Wright Music Co. Ltd. Lines from the songs, 'Oh! It's a Lovely War', 'There's a Long, Long Trail', 'It's a Long, Long Way to Tipperary' and the soldiers' parody 'Hush, here comes a Whizzbang' ('Hush, here comes the Dream Man') are reproduced by permission of B. Feldman & Co. Ltd.

Oh What a Lovely War was first presented by Theatre Workshop at the Theatre Royal, Stratford, London E15, on 19th March 1963, with the following cast:

The Pierrots

Ann Beach	**Griffith Davies**
Fanny Carby	**John Gower**
Bettina Dickson	**Colin Kemball**
Myvanwy Jenn	**Murray Melvin**
	Brian Murphy
Barry Bethell	**George Sewell**
Brian Cronin	**Victor Spinetti**
Larry Dann	**Bob Stevenson**

The play was subsequently presented at the Wyndham's Theatre, London (first performance 20th June 1963) with the following cast:

Avis Bunnage	**John Gower**
Fanny Carby	**Tony Holland**
Judy Cornwell	**Godfrey James**
Myvanwy Jenn	**Colin Kemball**
Mary Preston	**Murray Melvin**
	Brian Murphy
Barry Bethell	**Joseph Powell**
Larry Dann	**George Sewell**
Griffith Davies	**Victor Spinetti**
George Giles	**Bob Stevenson**

A Theatre Workshop Group Production
under the direction of **Joan Littlewood**
Setting by John Bury
Choroeography by Bob Stevenson
Costumes by Una Collins

The photographs show scenes from the original production.
Photographs: Roman Cagnoni (Report)

Cast

In alphabetical order

Alice Bailey Johnson
Ian Bartholomew
Alex Giannini
Oliver J. Hembrough
Rebecca Howell
Tom Lorcan
Ciarán Owens
Shaun Prendergast
Caroline Quentin
Zoe Rainey
Kyle Redmond-Jones
Michael Simkins
Understudies
Marcus Ellard
Leanne Harwood

Band

Musical Director/Piano
MIKE DIXON
Trumpet/Cornet/Flugel
Graham Justin
Drums/Percussion
Ryan Martin
Cello **Llinos Richards**
Double Bass **Frazer Snell**

Creative Team

Directed by **Terry Johnson**
Designed by **Lez Brotherston**
Musical Supervision &
   Musical Arrangements
   Mike Dixon

Choreography **Lynne Page**
Lighting Design
   Paul Pyant
Sound Design **Mike Walker**
Video Design
   Ian William Galloway
Casting Director
   Pippa Ailion

Production

Associate Director
   Melanie Hillyard
Associate Choreographer
   Rebecca Howell
Associate Video Designer
   Leo Flint
Assistant Director
   Marcus Ellard
Assistant Designer
   Colin Falconer
Assistant Video Designer
   Bella Riza
Accent Coach
   Richard Ryder
Drill Consultant
   Sergeant Luke Stroud
Production Manager
   Richard Bullimore
Costume Supervisor **Ed Parry**
Prop Buyer **Marie Costa**
Company & Stage Manager
   theatre royal stratford east
Deputy Stage Manager
   Alison Pottinger

Assistant Stage Manager **Surenee Chan Somchit**
Assistant Stage Manager **Cleo Maynard**
Stage Management Placement **Stephen Freeman**
Dresser **Tamima Kirk**
Costume Assistant/Intern **Annelies Henny**
Wardrobe Intern **Rachel Croft**
Lighting Programmer **Jess Glaisher**
Production Electrician **Liam Cleary**
Production Sound Engineers **Chris Simpson** **Ryan Griffin** **Josh Richardson** **Charlie Smith**
Crew **Tim Trotman**
Follow Spot **Charlotte Mayhew**
Sound desk supplied by **Cadac**
Costume makers **Pat Farmer**

Sasha Keir
Clare Ramsell
Theatre Royal Stratford East
Wardrobe Department
Set built and painted by **Factory Settings**
Drape Refurbishment by **Ken Creasey**
Lighting supplied by **White Light**
Video supplied by **XL Video**
Sound supplied by **Loh Humm Audio**
Wigs Supplied by **Darren Ware @ The Wig Room**
Costumes Hire **Khaki Devils & National Theatre**
Costume Hire
Production Photography **Nobby Clark**
Film courtesy of the **Trustees of the Imperial War Museum**

Contents

Introduction

This is not a conventional play and will not come to life if treated as such. It was first performed by a company of fifteen skilled dancers and singers, accustomed to improvisation and guided by a director.

The idea came from Gerry Raffles, who had heard a BBC programme of songs from the First World War, the plot from Joan Littlewood, and the rest was worked out with the company. The first discussion went well until a recording of the radio programme was played to them.

'Terrible!'

'Sentimental.'

'All that feeling and no imagination.'

'Pure nostalgia.'

'It's not the songs, it's the way they're sung!' said Gerry. The BBC Singers, who'd attended this first session, left.

'They couldn't sing like that stuck in a trench!' said Griffith Davies.

'Waiting for the next bomb to blow their heads off,' said Ann Beach.

'Dirty ... lousy ... hungry ...' The company was awake now.

'And we never get up till the sergeant brings our breakfast up to bed.' It was Vic Spinetti singing. He'd had a taste of army life and that set the ball rolling. First one, then another had some story to tell, a story that had been handed down in the family, part of our national heritage.

We raided the local libraries, dug out facts and figures. A neighbour brought in a little tin box, with Princess Mary's profile stamped on the lid.

'It was my grandfather's – had cigarettes in it for Christmas – the princess sent them all one.'

Our story began to take shape. We had some taboos. No khaki on the stage. Even the word makes you think of war. No deaths.

What will we wear then? Pierrots were all the go in those

days. They'd perform on a platform set up on the beach, seats
3d. and 6d. Little red and blue bulbs would light up for the
evening show. Their costumes were white with black bobbles
and ruffs. Each costume was different to suit the style of the
performer. And they could all sing and dance and make you
laugh. They were the great joy of the seaside.

'Let's play our *Lovely War* as a Pierrot show.'

'And the girls?' cried Fanny Carby.

'Tiny crinolines and long black lace pants, caught in at the
ankle –'

'And we must have pretty hats and head-dresses – and
drapes for some of the scenes.'

'Sure.'

'And the fellers?' said Brian Murphy.

'You can change your Pierrot hats for helmets as the war
wears on. Medals and stripes can be attached with Velcro. The
weaponry's a problem.'

'No weaponry, please,' said Myvanwy.

'We'll make it ourselves, but it must look real.'

'I suppose we'll play on a bare stage,' said John Bury, our
designer.

'Sure . . . but we could use a couple of balconies, one above
the prompt corner, the other O.P. They can take the coloured
bulbs that light up for festive scenes.'

Essential to the play:

> A large screen, flown in and out, behind the acting area, on
> which slides of photographs taken during that war were
> projected to counterpoint the words of the songs.

> A newspanel which traversed the stage on which the names
> of battles appeared, followed by the number of those killed
> and wounded and the number of yards gained or lost.

> The Pierrots, the screen and the newspanel must all be in
> the same field of vision. If either the newspanel or the screen
> is suspended elsewhere, at the side of the auditorium for
> example, the audience will simply not look at them.

> The only furniture: four truncated cones used as seats.

And a few tips for the performers:

No 'put on' accents. If you can't use somebody else's easily, use your own but take great care with the pronunciation of French and German if you don't want to sound like Field-Marshal Sir John French! The actor playing the Drill Sergeant must invent his own language. That used by a real drill sergeant who came to put the actors through their paces, was too repetitively obscene for delicate ears.

Play in the present tense. Avoid declaiming. Cut emotion. Find the action in a speech. Throw out your ad libs after one usage. However good they were, there are plenty more where they came from. Don't slow down.

This new edition attempts to restore the life of the play to my memory of the first production at Stratford East in 1963. It cuts the excrescences that crept in after the original cast dispersed, revives the flattened dialogue, and clarifies the inadequate, sometimes misleading, stage directions. I wish you well with your production.

Joan Littlewood 2000

Oh What a Lovely War

Act One

OVERTURE

Newspanel　SUMMER 1914. SCORCHING BANK HOLIDAY FORECAST . . . GUNBOAT SMITH FOULS CARPENTIER IN SIXTH ROUND . . . OPERA BLOSSOMS UNDER THOMAS BEECHAM.

The company stroll on, in their own time, towards the end of the overture. They smile, wave at someone in the audience or just take their place, sit quietly and chat among themselves. The **M.C.** *enters, wearing a mortar board. He ad libs with the audience. When ready, he announces the opening number, 'Johnny Jones'.*

Band　　　　　ROW, ROW, ROW

The mime to the song represents a day on the river. Two **Pierrots** *hold a light blue drape across the stage about 6 inches high. On the intro, one of them runs across with one end. Another* **Pierrot** *takes a pole and punts across the stage. A fourth 'swims', balancing himself on a minute platform on wheels. The rest mime while they sing on the imaginary bank upstage:*

Song　　　　　ROW, ROW, ROW

Young Johnny Jones he had a cute little boat
And all the girlies he would take for a float.
He had girlies on the shore,
Sweet little peaches, by the score –
But master Johnny was a wise 'un, you know,

His steady girl was Flo
And every Sunday afternoon
She'd jump in his boat
And they would spoon.

Chorus   And then he'd row, row, row,
Way up the river he would row, row, row,
A hug he'd give her
Then he'd kiss her now and then,
She would tell him when,
They'd fool around and fool around
And then they'd kiss again.
And then he'd row, row, row,
A little further he would row, oh, oh, oh, oh
Then he'd drop both his oars,
Take a few more encores,
And then he'd row, row, row.

(Repeat the chorus until . . .)

A little further he would row, oh, oh, oh, oh
Then we'll drop both our oars,
Take a round of applause,
And then we'll go, go, go.

M.C.   Off and change! (*All except the* **M.C.** *go off. The*
M.C. *picks up a ringmaster's whip. Keep this ad lib fresh.*) Good
evening, all: seat for you here, darling. Any more? Right;
close the doors. Welcome to our little pierrot show; 'The
Merry Roosters'. We've got songs for you, a few battles
and some jokes. I've got the whip to crack in case you
don't laugh. (*To the* **Pierrots**.) Are you ready?

Pierrots   No!

M.C.   Good. Time for a joke. (*These two must be*
throwaways.) Did you hear the one about the German
Admiral Graf Von and his three daughters, Knit Von,
Pearl Von, and Plain Von. You should have laughed at
that; it was the best gag in the show. [*Or:* I'm glad you
laughed at that 'cos it's the worst gag in the show.] Shall I
tell you another one? There were these two Generals went

paddling, you see; they were down at Southend and in the water, when one General looked at the other General and said, 'Good God, Reggie, your feet are filthy!' 'Damn it all, man,' said the other General, 'I wasn't here last year . . .' You see he couldn't get the soap . . . Oh, never mind. You ready now?

Pierrots   Yes!

M.C.   Good. Milords, ladies and gentlemen, we will now perform for you the ever-popular War Game!

Band   MARCH OF THE GLADIATORS

Circus Parade: it is led by a **Pierrot**, *cartwheeling.* **France** *wears an officer's cap, a sexy woman either side of him;* **Germany**, *a helmet and leather belt; beside him,* **Austria**, *a girl with two yellow plaits hanging from her hat.* **Ireland** *leads the British group, wearing a green wrap-over skirt. She jigs along.* **Great Britain**, *wearing a sun helmet, rides on a man's back. A character in a turban holds a square, tasselled sunshade over them. Two* **Russians**, *wearing fur hats, dance along. This parade must keep moving and not stop to let the performers declaim.*

Newspanel   TROOPS FIRE ON DUBLIN CROWD — AUG 1. BRITISH CABINET VOTE AGAINST HELPING FRANCE IF WAR COMES — LIBERALS VOTE FOR NEUTRALITY UNDER ANY CIRCUMSTANCES — GERMANY SENDS 40,000 RIFLES TO ULSTER.

M.C. (*as the nations pass*)   La Belle France – Upright, steadfast Germany – Good morning, sir – The first part of the game is called 'Find the Thief'.

Band   A PHRASE OF LAND OF HOPE AND GLORY

Britain   Look here, we own 30 million square miles of colonies. The British Empire is the most magnificent example of working democracy the world has ever seen.

Voice   Hear absolutely hear.

M.C.   And the lady on my right.

Band   SI LE VIN EST BON

Frenchwoman   La République.

Frenchman   The seat of reason, the centre of world
civilisation – culture, and l'amour.

M.C.   They're at it again. Stop it. If they're not doing
that, they're eating. How big's your acreage?

Frenchwoman   Six million square kilometres.

M.C.   And you?

Band   A PHRASE OF DEUTSCHLAND ÜBER ALLES

Kaiser   Germany – a mere three million square
kilometres. But we are a new nation united only since
1871.

Frenchman   When you stole Alsace-Lorraine.

Kaiser   Ours, German.

M.C.   Hey, we haven't started to play the game yet.

Kaiser   We are a disciplined, moral, industrious people.
We want more say in the world's affairs.

M.C.   Have to keep an eye on you … (*To the* **Band**.)
Let's have the Russian Anthem.

Band   A PHRASE OF RUSSIAN ANTHEM

Russia   They're all Yids.

Newspanel   CHURCHILL ORDERS FLEET TO SCAPA FLOW.

M.C. (*to audience*)   The second part of the War Game. The
Plans.

Band   GERMAN MUSIC

Kaiser   War is unthinkable. It is out of the question.

Frenchman   It would upset the balance of power.

Britain   It would mean the ruin of the world,
undoubtedly.

Frenchman   Besides, our alliances make us secure.

Kaiser   But if you threaten us, then we have the supreme deterrent, which we will not hesitate to use . . .

M.C.   Ssh.

The **M.C.** *whistles. The stage darkens and the screen comes down. Everyone leaves but the* **Kaiser** *and* **Austria**. **General Moltke** *enters.* **Russia**, **France**, *and* **Britain** *listen as if hiding.*

Slide 1: Map showing the Schlieffen plan of 1914 for an attack on Paris.

Moltke (*with a pointer to the map*)   The German Army will win this battle by an envelopment with the right wing, and let the last man brush the Channel with his sleeve.

Kaiser   Violate the neutrality of Belgium and the Netherlands?

Moltke   World power or downfall. Liège twelve days after mobilisation M. Day, Brussels M.19, French frontier M.22, and we will enter Paris at 11.30 on the morning of M.39. I send all the best brains in the War College into the Railway Section.

Kaiser   And the Russians?

Moltke   They won't be ready till 1916.

M.C. (*whistles*)   Time's up.

Band   SI LE VIN EST BON

Slide 2: Map showing the French 'Plan 17' of 1914 for a French offensive.

Frenchman   France admits no law but the offensive. Advance with all forces to attack the German Army. France, her bugles sounding, her soldiers armed for glory, her will to conquer. An idea and a sword. Besides, they will attack Russia first.

Slide 3: Russian infantry marching with rifles.

1st Russian   The Russian steam roller. We have a million and a half bayonets. Better than bullets any day. Once in motion, we go rolling forward inex – (*He hiccups.*)

M.C.   Inexorably! The bar's open. Go and have a vodka.

M.C.   *blows bo'sun's pipe.*

Slide 4: A British battleship berthed at a pier.

Band   A PHRASE OF THE SONS OF THE SEAS

British Admiral   Well done. In the event of a war, the Royal Navy will keep more than a million Germans busy. We shall disembark on a ten-mile strip of hard sand on the northern shores of Prussia and draw off more than our weight of numbers from the fighting line. The overwhelming supremacy of the British Navy is the only thing to keep the Germans out of Paris.

M.C.   Hear, hear.

British General   On a point of order, sir, your plans appear to have little in common with those of the Army.

British Admiral   Look here, you soldiers are a pretty grotesque lot with your absurd ideas about war. Happily you are powerless. We could go right ahead and leave you to go fooling around the Vosges. Have you got a plan?

British General   Of course.

Slide 5: A blank.

British Admiral   Yes, I thought so.

The **Company** *intone the words: 'Peace in our time O Lord.'*
M.C.   *blows whistle.*

M.C.   Any questions so far? Got all the plans off? Good. Can't help you any more. I want to watch the next scene.

Newspanel   SARAJEVO.

Band   SMETANA: RICHARD III

M.C.   Lovely music, Smetana.

The music is the gentle phrase to go with the mood of a sunny afternoon promenade in the park at Sarajevo. The ladies look pretty in hats, gloves and sunshades with soft colours added to their Pierrot costume. A tiny dog is being walked by his mistress, he wears a rather large bow. Army officers salute the ladies en passant. A junior one is ousted by his senior. One wears a straw boater with a pale blue ribbon but he cuts no ice at all. A pistol shot and a roll of thunder break the atmosphere. Everybody runs for cover. A beer stall with a small portrait of the Archduke Ferdinand hanging on it is pushed on by a street vendor. Two drinkers keep up with the stall. They are in fact secret policemen in plain clothes.

Serbian Secret Policeman   Ein dunkles Bier, bitte.

Austro-Hungarian Secret Policeman   Did you hear anything?

Serbian   You mean that shot?

Austro-Hungarian   Ja.

Serbian   No, I heard nothing.

Austro-Hungarian   I'll have a Bier, please.

Serbian   Lovely weather we're having.

Austro-Hungarian   Ja, ja, very good.

Serbian   You say somebody shot somebody?

Austro-Hungarian   Ja, ja, the Archduke Ferdinand, the fat one.

Serbian   No.

Austro-Hungarian   Ja.

Serbian   Who did he shoot?

Austro-Hungarian   No, he was shot.

Serbian   Do they know who did it?

Austro-Hungarian   That is the question.

*The **Stallholder** takes down the picture of the Archduke.*

He was driving a motor car.

Serbian   Very dangerous things, motor cars.

Austro-Hungarian   With the Archduchess.

Serbian   Big fat Sophie.

The **Austro-Hungarian** *starts taking notes.*

Austro-Hungarian   Ja, big fat Sophie. With a revolver.

Serbian   Should have used a pistol. A Browning automatic. With a Browning automatic you can shoot twenty archdukes.

Austro-Hungarian   Do you know who did it? (*To* **Stallholder**.) Do you know who did it?

Stallholder   No. I never meddle in politics.

Austro-Hungarian   Then what have you done with the Archduke Ferdinand's portrait?

Stallholder   I had to take it down. The flies shit all over it.

Serbian   I will tell you exactly who did it.

Austro-Hungarian   Yes?

Serbian   It was either a Catholic, a Protestant, a Jew, or a Serb, or a Croat, or a young Czech Liberal, or an Anarchist, or a Syndicalist. In any case it means war.

Austro-Hungarian   You think so?

Serbian   Of course. 'Bong!,' says Austria, 'Shoot my nephew, would you? There's one in the schmackers for you.' Then in comes Kaiser Willie to help Austria, in comes Russia to help Serbia, and in comes France because they hated Germany since 1871.

Austro-Hungarian (*writing on a pad*)   '. . . because they hated Germany since 1871.' Very good, thank you. Would you sign this please?

Serbian (*signing*)   This war has been coming for a long time.

Austro-Hungarian Ja, I am glad you think so. Step out on to the pavement. I am a member of the Austro-Hungarian Secret Police.

Serbian And I am a member of the Serbian Secret Police.

Austro-Hungarian Ah! We liquidated you yesterday – I arrest you for high treason.

Serbian What about him?

Austro-Hungarian Good idea. We arrest you.

Stallholder But I've said nothing!

Austro-Hungarian You said the flies could scheister on the Kaiser. Left, right, left, right . . . (*As they move off.*)

Serbian This means war.

Band   TWELFTH STREET RAG

All three go off. The music is fast and excited. People's hearts are beating. Two **Newsboys** *run across the stage.*

First Newsboy Special! Austria declares war on Serbia!

Second Newsboy Extra! Russia mobilises! Russia mobilises!

Two **Girls** *cross the stage pushing a tandem bicycle.*

First Girl Russia mobilises?

Second Girl Ja, and Papa says France must stand by Russia.

First Girl Oh! Is that good?

Two **German Businessmen** *pass with bowler hats and dispatch-cases.*

First Businessman I understand that we have ordered Russia to demobilise within twelve hours. The point is, will France remain neutral?

Second Businessman   Russia is asking for time.

First Businessman   Where did you hear that?

Second Businessman   It's all over town.

First Businessman   War's off, then?

Second Businessman   Yes. War is off.

First Businessman   Good. Otto, Otto, the war is off.

Cheering. Music. A female **Ballet Dancer** *enters, dancing. She is beckoned off by someone in the wings. She goes. After a few seconds she returns and holds up her hand. The music stops.*

Dancer   Damen und Herren, the German ultimatum to Russia has expired.

The screen is flown out. A Big Ben clock strikes one. Everybody around comes onstage and stands still, listening.

German Herald (*on a balcony at the side of the stage*)   Ich bestimme hiermit, das Deutsche Heer und die Kaiserliche Marine, sind nach Massgabe des Mobilmachungsplans für das Deutsche Heer und die Kaiserliche Marine kriegsbereit aufzustellen. Der Zweite August 1914 wird als erster Mobilmachungstag festgesetzt. Berlin Ersten August 1914. Wilhelm König von Preussen und Deutscher Kaiser. Bethman Hollweg (Reichskanzler).

The sound of trains stopping can be heard behind the following announcements.

Female Station Announcer   All civilian trains cancelled.

Male Station Announcer   All civilian trains cancelled.

Female Station Announcer   Until further notice, there will be no more passenger trains leaving this station.

Male Station Announcer   Until further notice, there will be no more passenger trains leaving this station.

The **Kaiser** *enters with* **Moltke**.

Kaiser   The world will be engulfed in the most terrible of wars, the ultimate aim of which is the ruin of Germany. England, France and Russia have conspired together for our annihilation.

Moltke   France has mobilised, Your Majesty.

Kaiser   The encirclement of Germany is an accomplished fact. We have run our heads into a noose. England?

Moltke   They have not yet made up their minds.

Kaiser   Abandon the Plan.

Moltke   It is too late. The wheels are already in motion.

Kaiser   Send a telegram to my cousin George V, notifying him my troops are being prevented by telephone and telegram from passing through Belgium.

Two **Soldiers** *with field telephones run on and sit at opposite sides of the stage. By now French, German and English military caps should be worn. Sound of morse tapping.*

Frenchman   War might burst from a clump of trees – a meeting of two patrols – a threatening gesture – a black look – a brutal word – a shot.

Englishman (*from a balcony*)   The lamps are going out all over Europe. We shall not see them lit again in our lifetime.

English Soldier   'Ere – they've gone into Luxembourg.

Luxembourg Soldier   Notify England, France, Belgium, a platoon of Germans has gone into Luxembourg.

Kaiser   Notify Lieutenant Feldmann that he is to withdraw immediately from Luxembourg.

English Soldier   No, it is a mistake.

Moltke   Advance into Luxembourg.

Kaiser   Advance.

Luxembourg Soldier   Platoon withdrawn.

English Soldier   They've gone in all right . . . eh? . . .

Blimey! We're off! They've crossed into Belgium an' all!

Explosion. The lights go out. Full stage lighting flashes on. The whole **Company** *is standing in a semicircle grinning and clapping wildly but soundlessly. The band plays a line of the National Anthem. All the* **Pierrots** *stand to attention.*

M.C. (*quietly and seriously*)   Will the lady in the second row kindly remove that dachshund.

The **Pierrots** *move to go off. The* **Band** *plays a line of 'The Marseillaise'. They move to go off again. The* **Band** *plays a line of the Belgian Anthem (two-thirds through). Nobody knows it. They turn to watch the newspanel.*

Newspanel   AUG 4 BRITAIN DECLARES WAR ON GERMANY.

The **M.C.** *blows a whistle. The screen comes down.*

M.C.   Well, that's the end of Part One of the War Game.

The **Band** *plays a chorus of 'Your King and Country', during which the* **Pierrots** *go off one by one, as slides of the coming of war in different countries are shown, ending up with the Kitchener poster.*

Slide sequence:
Slide 5: British civilian volunteers, marching in column of fours from recruiting office.
Slide 6: Street parade of civilians led by young boys, one with Union Jack and another playing the bagpipes.
Slide 7: Crowd of German civilians cheering a military parade.
Slide 8: Another parade of British civilians being led by young boys, one with Union Jack, another playing a drum.
Slide 9: Young British girls dancing in the streets.
Slide 10: Crowd of British volunteers outside a recruiting office.
Slide 11: Eton schoolboys marching with rifles at the slope.
Slide 12: Poster of Kitchener pointing, with caption 'Your Country Needs You'.

The **Girls** *sing.*

Song   YOUR KING AND COUNTRY

We've watched you playing cricket
And every kind of game.

At football, golf and polo,
You men have made your name.
But now your country calls you
To play your part in war,
And no matter what befalls you,
We shall love you all the more.
So come and join the forces
As your fathers did before.

Oh, we don't want to lose you but we think you ought
to go
For your king and your country both need you so.
We shall want you and miss you but with all our might
and main,
We shall cheer you, thank you, kiss you,
When you come back again.

The **Band** *plays a half-chorus of the song. Mime tableau showing* **Belgium** *kneeling and* **Germany** *threatening with bayonet.* **Austria***, the girl in plaits, is lost, pleading in between.*

M.C.   Gallant little Belgium.

The chorus is repeated during which there is a mime of recruiting. The **Men** *hand in their Pierrot hats and kiss the* **Girls** *goodbye, marching off behind the screen.*
They re-emerge wearing uniform caps and marching off saluting.

Newspanel   COURAGE WILL BRING US VICTORY.

Band   CAVALRY CHARGE MUSIC

Six **Men***, wearing the capes and caps of the French cavalry enter upstage, riding imaginary horses.*

Standard-Bearer   Bonjour, mes amis.

French Soldier   Bonjour, mon capitaine.

Standard-Bearer   Il fait beau pour la chasse . . . Vive la République!

French Officer   En avant!

They gallop downstage. There is a sound of gunfire: an ambush. They retreat.

Standard-Bearer   Maintenant mes amis!

French Soldier   Ah oui.

Standard-Bearer   Pour la gloire.

French Officer   Charge!

Band   PART OF THE MARSEILLAISE

The cavalry charge. There is a sound of machine-gun fire and whinnying horses. The **Men** *are killed and collapse.*
They hold their poses, standing, sitting or lying while a **Girl** *enters, wearing a braided military style jacket and a shako. She sings briskly and triumphantly.*

Newspanel   GERMANS HELD AT LIÈGE . . . LONDON WILD WITH JOY.

Band   WHEN BELGIUM PUT THE KIBOSH ON THE KAISER

A silly German sausage
Dreamt Napoleon he'd be,
Then he went and broke his promise,
It was made in Germany.
He shook hands with Britannia
And eternal peace he swore,
Naughty boy, he talked of peace
While he prepared for war.
He stirred up little Serbia
To serve his dirty trick
But naughty nights at Liège
Quite upset this Dirty Dick.
His luggage labelled 'England'
And his programme nicely set,
He shouted 'First stop Paris',
But he hasn't got there yet.

For Belgium put the kibosh on the Kaiser;
Europe took a stick and made him sore;
On his throne it hurts to sit,
And when John Bull starts to hit,

He will never sit upon it any more.

His warships sailed upon the sea,
They looked a pretty sight
But when they heard the bulldog bark
They disappeared from sight.
The Kaiser said 'Be careful,
If by Jellicoe they're seen,
Then every man-of-war I've got
Will be a submarine'.
We chased his ships to Turkey,
And the Kaiser startled stood,
Scratch'd his head and said 'Don't hurt,
You see I'm touching wood';
Then Turkey brought her warships
Just to aid the German plot,
Be careful, Mr Turkey,
Or you'll do the Turkey Trot.

Belgium put the kibosh on the Kaiser;
Europe took a stick and made him sore;
And if Turkey makes a stand
She'll get gurkha'd and japanned,
And it won't be Hoch the Kaiser any more.

He'll have to go to school again
And learn his geography,
He quite forgot Britannia
And the hands across the sea,
Australia and Canada,
The Russian and the Jap,
And England looked so small
He couldn't see her on the map.
Whilst Ireland seemed unsettled,
'Ah' said he 'I'll settle John',
But he didn't know the Irish
Like he knew them later on.
Though the Kaiser stirred the lion,
Please excuse him from the crime,
His lunatic attendant
Wasn't with him at the time.

The cavalry rise and join in. All sing:

> Belgium put the kibosh on the Kaiser;
> Europe took a stick and made him sore;
> We shall shout with victory's joy,
> Hold your hand out, naughty boy,
> You must never play at soldiers any more.

> For Belgium put the kibosh on the Kaiser;
> Europe took a stick and made him sore;
> On his throne it hurts to sit,
> And when John Bull starts to hit,
> He will never sit upon it any more.

All go off, except for one **French Officer** *who sits on stage writing a letter.*

Newspanel   BRUSSELS FALLS.

French Officer (*with quiet sincerity*)   The battlefield is unbelievable; heaps of corpses, French and German, lying everywhere, rifles in hand. Thousands of dead lying in rows on top of each other in an ascending arc from the horizontal to an angle of sixty degrees. The guns recoil at each shot; night is falling and they look like old men sticking out their tongues and spitting fire. The rain has started, shells are bursting and screaming; artillery fire is the worst. I lay all night listening to the wounded groaning. The cannonading goes on; whenever it stops we hear the wounded crying from all over the woods. Two or three men go mad every day.

The **French Officer** *goes off. A* **German Officer** *is discovered on the opposite side of the stage, reading a letter.*

German Officer   Nothing more terrible could be imagined; we advanced much too fast. The men are desperately tired. I feel great pity for many of the civilian population, who have lost everything, but they hate us. One of them fired at us; he was immediately taken out and shot. Yesterday we were ordered to attack the enemy flank in a forest of beeches, but the enemy gunners saw us and opened fire; the men were done for, the shells fell like hail.

He goes off. **Pierrots** *in army caps march on, accompanied by the* **Girl** *who sang 'Kibosh', still wearing her braided jacket and shako. She conducts them as they sing.*

Song   ARE WE DOWNHEARTED?

Are we downhearted? No.
Then let your voices ring and all together sing
Are we downhearted? No.
Not while Britannia rules the waves, not likely;
While we've Jack upon the sea, and Tommy on the land
    we needn't fret.
It's a long, long way to Tipperary, but we're not
    downhearted yet.

She turns towards the audience to sing.

Song   HOLD YOUR HAND OUT, NAUGHTY BOY

Hold your hand out, naughty boy.
Hold your hand out, naughty boy.
Last night, in the pale moonlight,
I saw you, I saw you;
With a nice girl in the park,
You were strolling full of joy,
And you told her you'd never kissed a girl before:
Hold your hand out, naughty boy.

As this song begins, four young couples enter from the four corners of the stage. The **Girls** *have pretty bits, a flower in the hair, pretty gloves, a posy at the wrist. One has a sunshade. Three of the* **Young Men** *wear straw boaters, two carry canes, one is bareheaded but he has a black and white umbrella. They stroll about and choose a moment to kiss their partner, hiding their faces behind their hats. The bareheaded one merely blows a kiss.*

Band   FEW BARS OF SMASH-UP RAG

The change of tempo brings on the **Drill Sergeant** *and scatters the* **Pierrots** *in army caps. The* **'Kibosh Girl'** *waves at the* **Drill Sergeant**, *blows a kiss and goes.*

The **Drill Sergeant** *wears a Sergeant Major's cap and belt and has his trousers tucked into his socks. He carries a short stick. His* *number must be played in meaningful gibberish. He shouts at the four* **Young Men** *from the previous number "ifle d'ill'. They don't understand. He curses unintelligibly and repeats "ifle d'ill'.*

The nearest **Young Man** *carrying a cane says, 'We've no rifles.' This irritates the* **Drill Sergeant** *who indicates that in the army you use anything you can find. As he talks, he snatches the* **Young Man**'s *cane, tries to bend it and throws it back.*

1. He summons the **Young Men**. *Two come with walking canes, one with a sunshade and the bareheaded one has his umbrella.*

2. The **Drill Sergeant** *has them at attention in a straight line, explains the rifle, shows them how to carry it, over one shoulder; corrects their stance, is especially hard on the bareheaded one with the umbrella.*

3. Fix bayonets! He illustrates. It means holding the rifle between their thighs and fixing the imaginary bayonet. The **Umbrella One** *fumbles, exciting the* **Drill Sergeant** *to more vituperation. Is he a sissy? Where does he come from? Does he have a family?*

4. The lunge section: lunging and parrying to the left, to the right. More abuse. And do they know who the enemy is?

5. He creates as much hatred as he can. Maybe he's f—d your mother, your sister and your brother Go for his '—'. Ruin his chances. And he shows them how to lunge.

6. The Charge! They try. He is in despair. Tragic, he says. And exhorts them once more in the wildest of gibberish. ONCE MORE! he cries and they charge with some ferocity. The Umbrella one, now quite worked up, leaps into the audience and chases a **Programme Girl**, *who screams for help.*

7. The **Drill Sergeant** *recalls the* **Umbrella One**, *dubs him sex-mechanic and touches his cap to the* **Programme Girl**. *'Sorry, miss.' Then he turns on his recruits. 'Into line. Quick march. Left, Right. Left, Right.' And he marches them off. As they march off a* **Girl Singer** *enters. She sings, not with today's frank sexuality, but with the seductive splendour of the period.*
During the song the following slides are projected, at the points indicated by numbers in the text:

Slide 13: 1914 poster – 'Women of Britain say – "GO".'
Slide 14: 1914 poster – 'Everyone should do his bit – Enlist now' –
depicting a Boy Scout in uniform.
Slide 15: 1914 poster – 'Which? Have you a REASON – or only
an EXCUSE – for not enlisting NOW?'
Slide 16: 1914 poster – ' "Stand not upon the order of your going
but go at once" – Shakespeare – Macbeth 3.4. Enlist now.'
Slide 17: Poster – 'Who's absent? Is it YOU?' – depicting a line of
soldiers with John Bull in the foreground pointing accusingly à la
Kitchener.

Song   I'LL MAKE A MAN OF YOU

The Army and the Navy need attention, [13]
The outlook isn't healthy you'll admit,
But I've got a perfect dream of a new recruiting scheme,
Which I think is absolutely it.
If only other girls would do as I do
I believe that we could manage it alone,
For I turn all suitors from me but the sailor and the
   Tommy,
I've an army and a navy of my own.

On Sunday I walk out with a Soldier,
On Monday I'm taken by a Tar,
On Tuesday I'm out with a baby Boy Scout, [14]
On Wednesday a Hussar;
On Thursday I gang oot wi' a Scottie,
On Friday, the Captain of the crew;
But on Saturday I'm willing, if you'll only take the
   shilling,
To make a man of any one of you. [15]

I teach the tenderfoot to face the powder,
That gives an added lustre to my skin,
And I show the raw recruit how to give a chaste salute,
So when I'm presenting arms he's falling in.
It makes you almost proud to be a woman.
When you make a strapping soldier of a kid.
And he says 'You put me through it and I didn't want to
   do it
But you went and made me love you so I did.' [16]

Four **Girls** *enter, two from each side, and join in. They wear revealing sexy costumes and military headgear.*

On Sunday I walk out with a Bo'sun.
On Monday a Rifleman in green,
On Tuesday I choose a 'sub' in the 'Blues',
On Wednesday a Marine;
On Thursday a Terrier from Tooting,
On Friday a Midshipman or two,
But on Saturday I'm willing, if you'll only take the shilling,
To make a man of any one of you.

The **Band** *repeat the chorus.*

Singer   Come on, boys; we need a million.

First Girl   A million.

Singer   Be a man; enlist today.

Second Girl   Enlist today.

Singer   Have you a man digging your garden, when he should be digging trenches?

Third Girl   He should be digging trenches.

Singer   Have we any able-bodied men in the house?

Fourth Girl   Any able-bodied men?

Singer (*picking up the last line of the chorus*) . . . But on Saturday I'm willing, if you'll only take the shilling,
To make a man of any one of you.[17]

All go off.

An **Army Driver** *sets four cones to represent a car, upstage right. He salutes as* **Field-Marshal Sir John French**, *his* **Aide** *and* **Field-Marshal Sir Henry Wilson** *take their places and sit in the 'car'. The* **Driver** *starts it up. The sound of the car running and lurching accompanies the scene.*

Newspanel   THE ALLIES CONFER.

French   Right driver . . . (*They all bump up and down in their* *seats*.) Steady on there! One must always remember the class of people these French (*Another bump*.) these French generals come from . . .

Aide Yes, sir.

French Mostly tradesmen. Shan't understand a damn' word they say.

Aide With regard to that, sir, do you think I ought to organize an (*Another bump*.) an interpreter?

French Don't be ridiculous, Wilson; the essential problem at the moment is (*Another bump*.) is the utmost secrecy.

The car continues to run quietly, the light on it lowered. **General Lanrezac**, *his* **Aide** *and the Belgian* **General de Moranneville** *enter downstage left.* **Moranneville**'s *country, Belgium, is already lost.*

Lanrezac (*spreading his arms in a gesture of despair*) Personne! (*He strides up and down.*) Où se trouvent les Anglais? . . . Pour l'amour de Dieu, où sont-ils?

Moranneville Your turn to wait now, mon général.

Lanrezac (*to his* **Aide**) Qu'est-ce qu'il dit, le Belge?

French Aide Ce sont les Anglais que nous avons attendu longtemps.

Moranneville Belgium has had her share of waiting – when we held out at Liège hoping for the promised help – that never came.

Lanrezac En français, s'il vous plaît, monsieur. L'anglais je ne comprends pas.

Moranneville (*shrugging his shoulders*) Ça m'est égal!

He walks off contemptuously, leaving the other two to pace up and down. Lights up on the car.

Wilson I've actually worked out the number of carriages we'll need for the first stage, sir, and even the quantity of forage for the horses; wouldn't care to see the figures, would you?

French   No, no. (*They all lurch.*) Not just now, thank you.

Wilson   I thought that . . . considering the terrain . . .

French   Yes, yes, we all know about your bicycle rides round France, Wilson.

The car pulls up. They all lurch forward and back, then dismount.

Wilson (*moving forward enthusiastically*)   Mon cher Lanrezac. (*They clutch hands, almost embrace.*) Splendid! Splendide de vous revoir.

Lanrezac   Enchanté, mon général.

Wilson   May I present Field-Marshal Sir John French, Commander-in-Chief of the British Expeditionary Force?

Lanrezac   Bienvenu, monsieur.

French   How do you do, sir?

Lanrezac   Je vous présente le Général de Moranneville, Commandeur des Forces Belges.

French Belgian? (**Wilson** *nods.*) Splendid! Gallant little Belgium, what?

Lanrezac   Oui, mais malheureusement, comme d'habitude, vous êtes en retard. Vous avez l'heure?

French   What?

French Aide   You are 'ere, mon général, and not a moment too soon.

French   Dammit all, we came here as quickly as we could. You have damn' bad roads in France.

Lanrezac   Intéressant! Roads? Roads, 'e say? Ah oui, c'est la route maintenant! Que des excuses, toujours des excuses! Et si c'est la fin! Si la France est perdu, c'est à cause de vous. Oui! Dieu sait óu vous étiez –

French Aide   God knows where you have been. If France should be lost . . .

Lanrezac   Continuez, continuez.

French Aide   We owe it to you.

French   Dammit all! We're under no obligation.

Lanrezac (*to his* **Aide**)   Tu as traduit tout ce que j'ai dit?

French Aide   Oui, mon général, mot à mot.

Lanrezac (*angrily*)   Je suis à bout de patience. J'en ai assez. J'en ai assez.

French Aide   Je m'excuse, mon général.

Lanrezac   Tais toi!

He repeats himself angrily.

Wilson (*to* **French**)   I say sir, don't you think we need a translator?

French   Certainly not, Wilson. I can handle this perfectly on my own! (*To* **Lanrezac**.) Mon général, promenade s'il vous plaît.

Lanrezac (*snorts*)   Ah! On parle français maintenant.

French   Bit of an 'accent' (*French pronunciation.*), I'm afraid.

Lanrezac   Pas du tout, pas du tout.

French   Eh? (*He sees the* **French Aide** *looking at a map.*) Excusez-moi, s'il vous plaît. (*He beckons the* **Aide** *to give him the map.*) Merci. Thank you! (*To* **Lanrezac**.) Mon général, les Allemands . . .

Lanrezac   Oui, les Allemands. Je vous écoute, mon général.

French   Of course! Yes! Bien sûr. Les Allemands traversent − (*Aside to* **Wilson**.) What's 'cross the river', Wilson?

Wilson   Traverser le fleuve.

French   Of course! (*To* **Lanrezac**.) Traversent le fleuve . . . ici . . . ahoy, à Hoy.

Lanrezac   Je ne comprends pas. O-ie? O-ie?

French   That's it! Ici. Ahoy.

Lanrezac   Non, non, non, non! À Huy.

French   Ahoy.

Lanrezac   Huy! Ache. U. Ygrec.

French (*turns to* **Wilson**, *lost*)   What? Eh? What, what, what?

Wilson (*studying the map*)   Les Allemands traversent le fleuve à Huy, n'est-ce pas?

Lanrezac   Oui! Mais peut-être pour aller à la pêche.

French Aide   Perchance they will go fishing . . .

French (*laughing*)   Most amusin'.

Wilson   I think he means to say that the Germans will probably cross the river here, at the bridge.

French   Of course, yes, of course. Plain as the nose on your face. Très bon, très bon! In that case, gentlemen, we will hold one division, une division, guarding the bridge – le pont – là; and another division will be held in reserve, by the clump of trees, le clump des arbres, là, and the French cavalry will govern the sector from there to there! Là à là.

Lanrezac   Ah! Très bien! La cavalerie française doit porter le fardeau, comme d'habitude! Non! Ce n'est pas possible. Je n'accepte pas! Vous êtes en guerre, monsieur? Les Anglais sont en guerre, non?

French   Yes! Oui! But we only have four divisions, my dear sir, not the six promised by Kitchener. The English cavalry must be kept in reserve.

Lanrezac   Et le B.E.F.? Où se trouve le B.E.F.?

He walks off.

French Aide   When may we expect the B.E.F. to come

into action, monsieur?

Lanrezac (*returning*) Le B.E.F., mon général! Le Breeteesh Expedeeshonaire Force!

French   All in good time, old chap, all in good time.

Lanrezac   Mais *quand*?

French   Soon as possible . . . the twenty-fourth!

French Aide   Le vingt-quatre, mon général.

Lanrezac   Et les Allemands? Ils vont attendre jusqu'au moment où le dernier bouton est trouvé? Bah!

He waves his arms angrily.

French   Dammit all, Wilson! This is no way to conduct a conference.

Wilson   No sir, sorry sir.

French   We're not here under any obligation.

Moranneville   May I remind both gentlemen that my country has already fallen. So far, to help us, we have received a visit from one staff officer – to observe. Decisive action by Britain – and France – while my troops were holding Liège, and the war would have been over by now. Adieu, gentlemen.

He goes.

French   Whatever our chaps can do, they will do! Which reminds me. Mon général, I have been entrusted by His Majesty, the King, to award you this medal. (*His* **Aide** *brings out a little box and opens it.* **French** *takes the medal and pins it on beside the array* **Lanrezac** *wears already.* **Lanrezac** *kisses* **French** *on both cheeks to the latter's embarrassment.* **French** *salutes.*)   Vive la France!

Lanrezac *and his* **Aide** *salute and go. Four young* **French Girls**, *bringing flowers, come running on. They give the flowers to* **French** *and* **Wilson**, *then hug and kiss the* **Driver**.

Girls   Bienvenus, les Anglais.

Band   MADEMOISELLE FROM ARMENTIÈRES

Wilson *and* **French** *go. The* **Driver** *dances off with the* **Girls**.

Newspanel   AUG 25 RETREAT FROM MONS. AUG 30 FIRST BRITISH WOUNDED ARRIVE AT WATERLOO.

Two **Women** *enter. The first wears a short, black shawl and carries a basket of violets, a single bunch in her spare hand. The second wears a man's cap and carries a bundle of newspapers.*

First Woman   Lovely violets . . .

Second Woman   *Star, News, Standard* . . . First wounded arrive at Waterloo . . . Read all about it.

First Woman   Lovely violets . . .

Second Woman   *Star, News, Standard* . . . First wounded arrive from France.

A **Sergeant** *and wounded* **Soldiers** *come on.*

Sergeant   Come on then, let's have you. Get yourself fell in. Mind your crutch . . . get moving.

First Soldier   No flags, sarg?

Sergeant   No.

First Soldier   Waterloo, boys, can you smell it?

Sergeant   Get yourselves in a straight line. (**Officers** *and* **Nurse** *enter.*) Eyes front.

First Soldier   They can't do that, can they, sarg? They haven't got any.

First Officer   Thank you, sergeant, carry on.

A **Corporal** *enters.*

Sergeant   Yes, corporal?

Corporal   Ambulances are ready, sarg. Officers only.

Sergeant   What about the other ranks?

Corporal   No arrangements made for them at the moment.

Sergeant   All right, carry on, corporal. (*Exit* **Corporal**. *To* **Officers**.) Excuse me, sir, if you care to step this way we have transport laid on for you.

First Officer   Nearly home, George. Thank you, sergeant.

Second Soldier   Sir, sir, Higgins, sir, B Company.

First Officer   Hallo, Higgins.

Second Soldier   Better than up the old Salient, eh, sir?

First Officer   Indeed yes, good journey home?

Second Soldier   Yes, thank you, sir.

First Officer   Chin up then. See you back at the front. (*Exit.*)

Second Soldier   Yes, sir.

First Soldier (*to the* **Nurse**, *who has been talking to the* **Second Officer** *and is helping him off.*) You're wasting your time with him, darling, it's in splints.

Sergeant   That's enough out of you.

Second Soldier   What about us then, sarg?

Sergeant   I'm waiting further orders.

The **Soldiers** *begin softly singing* 'WE'RE 'ERE BECAUSE WE'RE 'ERE', *getting louder.*

We're 'ere because we're 'ere, because we're 'ere, because we're 'ere,
We're 'ere because we're 'ere, because we're 'ere, because we're 'ere –

Sergeant   All right, cut it out.

George   What about a train back then, sarg.

Sergeant   You'll get that soon enough.

Corporal *enters.*

First Soldier Mafeking's been relieved, sarg.

Sergeant All right – corporal.

Corporal All arranged, sarg. Some lorry drivers outside have volunteered to take the men to Millbank Hospital in their dinner hour.

Sergeant Thank you, corporal, carry on . . . All right, men, get yourself fell in. We've got transport laid on for you. Come on now, pick 'em up, keep smiling, you're out of the war now.

Nurse (*to* **Stretcher Case**) Don't worry, we'll have you back in the firing line within a week.

Wounded Soldiers (*singing as they march off*)
Pack up your troubles in your old kit bag and smile,
    smile, smile,
While you've a lucifer to light your fag,
Smile boys that's the style. . . .

Newspanel 300,000 ALLIED CASUALTIES DURING AUGUST.

They begin to move off, the **Sergeant** *and* **Corporal** *last of all. A* **Girl Singer** *enters, a tray slung from her neck.*

Girl Chocolates, vanilla ices, bonbons. (*She offers the chocolate to the* **Sergeant**, *who declines as he moves off.*)

Slide 18 is projected and the following sequence during the
    song:
Slide 18: Poster – 'Carter's Little Liver Pills – for Active
    Service. For the Keen Eye of Perfect Health. Biliousness,
    Torpid Liver and Constipation.' Depicting a recruit
    stripped to the waist being examined by a Doctor.
Slide 19: Advertisement – 'PHOSFERINE The Greatest of
    All Tonics, Royalty Use Phosferine as a Liver Tonic,
    Blood Enricher, Nerve Strengthener.'
Slide 20: Advertisement – 'Beware of umbrellas made on
    German frames. When you Buy an Umbrella Insist on
    Having a Fox's frame. Entirely British made. Look for

these Marks. S. FOX & CO. LIMITED. PARAGON.'
Slide 21: Advertisement – 'IF YOU ARE RUN DOWN,
    TAKE BEECHAM'S PILLS.' Depicting a cyclist, who
    has just been run down by another cyclist.

Girl   Next week at this theatre, a special double bill: the
great American comedy Teddy Get Your Gun and He
Didn't Want to Do It, featuring What a Funk, the conchie.
Chocolates, vanilla ices, bonbons. (*Enter* **Male Dancer** *with
sheet music.*) Have you got your copy of Gwendoline
Brogden's latest hit – complete with pianoforte and banjo
parts included –

Song   HITCHY-KOO

Oh! Every evening hear him sing,
It's the cutest little thing,
With the cutest little swing,
Hitchy-koo, Hitchy-koo. [19]

Oh, simply meant for Kings and Queens,
Don't you ask me what it means,
I just love that Hitchy-koo,
Hitchy-koo, Hitchy-koo.

Say he does it just like no-one could,
When he does it say he does it good,
Oh, every evening hear him sing
It's the cutest little thing
With the cutest little swing,
Hitchy-koo, Hitchy-koo. [20]

Band *verse: Dance routine* [21].

Say he does it just like no-one could
When he does it say he does it good.
Oh, every evening hear him sing,
It's the cutest little thing,
With the cutest little swing,
Hitchy-koo, Hitch-koo, Hitchy-koo. . . .

As the **Singer** *and* **Partner** *go off, six* **British Soldiers**
come on, whistling and humming 'Hitchy-koo'. They set up signs

reading 'Piccadilly' (a fingerpost), 'Conducted tours of the German trenches', 'Apply to G.H.Q. 20 miles to the rear'. They settle within the area of the trench marked off by the signs, playing cards, writing, playing a mouth organ, etc.

Newspanel   TRENCH WARFARE BEGINS . . . THE FIRST WINTER.

First Soldier   Want a game?

Second Soldier   Yeah.

First Soldier   'Ere you are, you're banker.

The **Soldier** *with the mouth organ plays 'Clementine'.*

Third Soldier   Oi!

Fourth Soldier   What's 'e doin'?

Third Soldier   Writin' to 'is lady love.

Second Soldier   Blimey! Not agin.

Third Soldier   Third volume. My dearest, I waited for you two hours last night at 'Ellfire Corner, but you didn't turn up. Can it be that you no longer love me? Signed – Harry Hotlips.

Second Soldier   What's she like?

Fourth Soldier   Lovely.

Third Soldier   S'right. Only she's got a nose like a five-inch shell.

Fourth Soldier   Shut up, can't yer? I'm tryin' to concentrate.

Fifth Soldier   You writin' for that paper agin?

Fourth Soldier   Yeah, they don't seem to realise they're in at the birth of the Wipers Gazette. 'Ere, d'you want to 'ear what I've written?

Second Soldier   No.

Fourth Soldier (*to* **Fifth**)   Do you want to 'ear it?

Fifth Soldier   Yeah, go on.

Fourth Soldier   The Wipers Gazette. Agony column. Do you believe good news in preference to bad? Do you think the war will be over by spring-time? Have you got faith in our generals? If the answers to any of these questions is yes, then you are sufferin' from that dread disease, Optimism, and should take seven days' leave immediately.

First Soldier   Wish you'd take ten.

Fifth Soldier   Not a bad idea that paper.

Second Soldier   No, you want to get it framed.

Fifth Soldier   Yeah, put one in for me. Now the winter nights are drawin' in, wanted, cure for trench feet, corns, gripes . . .

First Soldier   Black or white?

Fifth Soldier   . . . chilblains and 'ow about some letters an' all – put that in.

Third Soldier   How about some Christmas parcels – put that in!

First Soldier   What's up with you, got company?

Sixth Soldier   Yeah. (*To his mates.*) Last time I went down to that delousin' station, they only shoved a hot iron over my trousers, came out with more than I went in with.

Sound of distant bombardment.

Fifth Soldier   Ssh. Listen.

Third Soldier   Yeah. They're coppin' it down Railway Wood tonight.

Sixth Soldier   That's Hill Sixty.

Fifth Soldier   No, not that. Listen.

A **German Soldier** *is heard singing. He should not be in the wings but at a distance consistent with the width of no man's land. The* **English** *and* **Germans** *calling to each other must suggest this distance.*

Song   HEILIGE NACHT

> Stille Nacht, heilige Nacht
> Alles schläft, einsam wacht,
> Nur das traute, hochheilige Paar.
> Holder Knabe im lockigen Haar,
> Schlaf in himmlischer Ruh'
> Schlaf in himmlischer Ruh'.

Second Soldier (*as the* **German** *sings*)   What is it?

Fifth Soldier   Singin'.

Third Soldier   It's those Welsh bastards in the next trench.

Fifth Soldier   No! That's Jerry.

First Soldier   It's an 'ymn.

Sixth Soldier   No – it's a carol.

Second Soldier   Wouldn't 'ave thought they 'ad 'em.

Third Soldier   It's Jerry all right, it's comin' from over there.

Fourth Soldier   Sings well for a bastard, don't 'e?

First Soldier   Sing up Jerry, let's 'ear yer!

Fifth Soldier   Put a sock in it! Listen.

They listen as 'Heilige Nacht' finishes.

Second Soldier   Nice, wasn't it? Good on yer, mate!

German Soldier   Hallo, Tommy! .... Hallo Tommy!

Fourth Soldier   'E 'eard yer.

Second Soldier   'Allo!

German Soldier   Wie geht's?

First Soldier   Eh?

German Soldier   How are you? I am very well senk you, good night.

First Soldier   Another day gone!

German Soldier   Hey, Tommy. How is it vis you?

English Soldiers   Lovely! Very good! Very well, thank you.

Third Soldier   Guten singin', Jerry!

Second Soldier   Got any more?

German Soldier   Fröhliche Weihnachten!

English Soldiers   Eh?

German Soldier   Good – Happy Christmas!

Second Soldier   Happy Christmas!

First Soldier   Hey! It's Christmas!

Fourth Soldier   No. Tomorrow.

Second Soldier (*to* **First Soldier**)   What about openin' your parcel?

First Soldier   I forgot it was Christmas.

German Soldier   Hallo Tommy!

English Soldiers   Yeah?

German Soldier   It is for you now to sing us a good song for Christmas, ja?

English Soldiers   Oh, ja!

Third Soldier   Let's give 'em onc.

Second Soldier   Go on, then!

Third Soldier   I can't sing.

First Soldier   We know that.

Fourth Soldier   Well, who's goin' to sing it?

Third Soldier (*to* **First Soldier**)   Give them that one of your'n.

First Soldier What – Cook'ouse?

English Soldiers Yeah!!

First Soldier All right, Jerry, get down in your dugout – it's comin' over!

He sings.

Song   CHRISTMAS DAY IN THE COOKHOUSE

It was Christmas day in the cook'ouse,
The 'appiest day of the year,
Men's 'earts were full of gladness
And their bellies full of beer,
When up spoke Private Short'ouse,
His face as bold as brass,
Saying, 'We don't want your Christmas puddin'
You can stick it up your —'

All Tidings of comfort and joy, comfort and joy,
Oh tidings of comfort and joy!

First Soldier It was Christmas day in the 'arem,
The eunuchs were standin' round,
And 'undreds of beautiful women
Was stretched out on the ground,
When in strolled the Bold Bad Sultan,
And gazed on 'is marble 'alls
Saying, 'What do you want for Christmas, boys?'
And the eunuchs answered '—'

All Tidings of comfort and joy, comfort and joy
Oh, tidings of comfort and joy.

Sound of **Germans** *applauding: 'Bravo Tommy.'*

Fourth Soldier Hey, listen.

German Soldier Bravo, Tommy. English carols is very beautiful! Hey, Tommy, present for you, coming over!

English Soldiers Watch out! Get down!

The **Soldiers** *dive for cover. A boot is thrown from the darkness upstage and lands in the trench.*

Third Soldier Quick, put a sandbag on it.

Sixth Soldier What is it?

Fifth Soldier It's a boot.

First Soldier Drop it in a bucket.

Fifth Soldier It's a Jerry boot.

Third Soldier What's that stickin' out of it?

Sixth Soldier It's a bit of fir tree.

First Soldier On a bit of ribbon.

Fifth Soldier Fags.

Fourth Soldier What's that?

Third Soldier That's chocolate, that is.

Second Soldier Is it?

Sixth Soldier Yeah.

English Soldiers Thanks Jerry – Good on yer, etc.

First Soldier That's German sausage.

Second Soldier Is it?

First Soldier Yeah.

Second Soldier It's yours.

Fifth Soldier Eh, we'll 'ave to send 'em somethin' back, won't we?

Second Soldier Come on then, get your parcel open.

First Soldier What about your'n then?

Second Soldier I ain't got one. They can 'ave my Christmas card from Princess Mary.

First Soldier 'Ere! What about the old girl's Christmas puddin'? Bet they've never tasted nuthin' like that before.

Third Soldier 'Ere y'are, I've been savin' this. My tin of cocoa – might make 'em sleep.

Fourth Soldier   Ain't got nothin', 'ave I?

Fifth Soldier   Right, Jerry, 'ere's your Christmas box.

He throws the boot.

German Soldier   Thanks, Tommy!

Explosion.

First Soldier   Blimey! The Christmas puddin' wasn't that strong.

German Soldier   Hey, Tommy! Are you still there?

English Soldiers   Just about, yeah. No thanks to you.

German Soldier   Many greetings to you, for your many presents and kindness to us, we thank you.

Second Soldier   You're very welcome.

First Soldier   That's all right.

German Soldier   Hey, you like to drink vis us, ja?

English Soldiers   Ja!

German Soldier   You like some Schnapps – good Deutsche Schnapps?

Fourth Soldier   Ja!! That's whisky!

English Soldiers   Yeah! Same thing! etc.

First Soldier   Sling it over!

German Soldier   We meet you! Meet you in the middle!

Fourth Soldier   Middle of Piccadilly?

First Soldier   See you in the penalty area! Good night, Jerry.

Second Soldier   Happy New Year, mate!

Third Soldier   They're marvellous linguists, you know.

Second Soldier   Oh yes, they learn it at school.

Fourth Soldier   I reckon I'll put that in the Gazette.

Fifth Soldier What?

Fourth Soldier About Jerry sendin' us a present.

Fifth Soldier Eh! Here! They're comin'.

The **German Soldiers** *appear upstage. The approach must be slow, tentative, both sides frightened of sudden death. The* **Germans** *must not appear too soon and even in the giving of the first present there is fear.*

First German Hallo, Tommy.

The **Third** *and* **Fifth British Soldiers** *go to meet the* **Germans**.

Second German Alles gut, ja.

He gives a bottle to the **Third British Soldier**.

Third Soldier Thanks very much.

Second German Bitte schön.

Fifth Soldier Hello, how are you?

Third Soldier Merry Christmas.

They shake hands, the others follow.

Second Soldier Hello, nice to see you – all right, are you? You should have come over before . . . Stone the crows, it was him saying good night.

They greet each other.

Newspanel ALL QUIET ON THE WESTERN FRONT . . . ALLIES LOSE 850,000 MEN IN 1914 . . . HALF BRITISH EXPEDITIONARY FORCE WIPED OUT.

During this message the **M.C.** *enters and the* **Soldiers** *turn to watch the newspanel in silence. The* **Soldiers** *pick up their signs and go off.*
The **M.C.** *sings 'Goodbye-ee' quietly and simply.*

Song   GOODBYE-EE

  Brother Bertie went away

To do his bit the other day
With a smile on his lips and his
Lieutenant's pips upon his shoulder bright and gay.
As the train moved out he said, 'Remember me to all
  the birds.'
And he wagg'd his paw and went away to war
Shouting out these pathetic words:

Goodbye-ee, goodbye-ee,
Wipe the tear, baby dear, from your eye-ee,
Tho' it's hard to part I know, I'll be tickled to death to
  go.
Don't cry-ee, don't sigh-ee, there's a silver lining in the
  sky-ee,
Bonsoir, old thing, cheer-i-o, chin, chin,
Na-poo, toodle-oo, Goodbye-ee.

The **Girls** *come on and join in. The last lines grow fainter as they
go off.*

Goodbye-ee, goodbye-ee,
Wipe the tear, baby dear, from your eye-ee,
Though it's hard to part I know, I'll be tickled to death
  to go.
Don't cry-ee, don't sigh-ee, there's a silver lining in the
  sky-ee . . .

Newspanel   WELCOME 1915 . . . HAPPY YEAR THAT WILL
BRING VICTORY AND PEACE.

Sound of shell exploding.
The last line of the song is inaudible.

CURTAIN

ENTR'ACTE

Act Two

Newspanel   APRIL 22 . . . BATTLE OF YPRES . . . GERMANS
USE POISON GAS . . . BRITISH LOSS 59,275 MEN . . . MAY 9 . . .
AUBERS RIDGE . . . BRITISH LOSS 11,619 MEN IN 15 HOURS . . .
LAST OF B.E.F. . . . GAIN NIL. SEPT 25 . . . LOOS . . . BRITISH
LOSS 8,236 MEN IN 3 HOURS . . . GERMAN LOSS NIL.

The company dressed as **Pierrots** *enter and sing.*

Song   OH IT'S A LOVELY WAR

Oh, oh, oh, it's a lovely war,
Who wouldn't be a soldier, eh?
Oh, it's a shame to take the pay;
As soon as reveille is gone,
We feel just as heavy as lead,
But we never get up till the sergeant
Brings our breakfast up to bed.
Oh, oh, oh, it's a lovely war,
What do we want with eggs and ham,
When we've got plum and apple jam?
Form fours, right turn,
How shall we spend the money we earn?
Oh, oh, oh, it's a lovely war.

Up to your waist in water,
Up to your eyes in slush,
Using the kind of language,
That makes the sergeant blush.
Who wouldn't join the army?
That's what we all inquire;
Don't we pity the poor civilian,
Sitting beside the fire.

Oh, oh, oh, it's a lovely war,
Who wouldn't be a soldier, eh?
Oh, it's a shame to take the pay;
As soon as reveille is gone,
We feel just as heavy as lead,
But we never get up till the sergeant
Brings our breakfast up to bed.
Oh, oh, oh, it's a lovely war,
What do we want with eggs and ham,
When we've got plum and apple jam?
Form fours, right turn,
How shall we spend the money we earn?
Oh, oh, oh, it's a lovely war.

M.C. Ladies and gentlemen, when the Conscription Act was passed, 51,000 able-bodied men left home without leaving any forwarding addresses . . .

Men *go off quickly.*

Girls Shame!

M.C. . . . and that's in West Ham alone.

As each of the **Girls** *speaks her line to the audience she throws a white feather.*

First Girl Women of England, do your duty, send your men to enlist today!

Second Girl Have you an able-bodied groom, chauffeur or gamekeeper serving you?

Third Girl If so, shouldn't he be serving his country?

Fourth Girl Is your best boy in khaki? if not shouldn't he be?

Fifth Girl What did you do in the Great War, Daddy?

Girls (*sing*) Oh, oh, oh, it's a lovely,
  Oh, oh, oh, it's a lovely,
  Oh, oh, oh, it's a lovely war!

Girls *exeunt.*

M.C. Sorry we had to interrupt the War Game in the first half, but hostilities took us by surprise; now it's business as usual – we'll drum up some char and we'll do part two of the War Game. What's the date?

Voice Off August the Twelfth.

M.C. August the Twelfth! Here am I talking to you when grouse shooting has commenced. (*Putting on a cloth cap.*) Whenever there's a crisis, shoot some grouse, that's what I always say. Here we are – part two of the War Game, find the biggest profiteer.

Newspanel 21,000 AMERICANS BECAME MILLIONAIRES DURING THE WAR.

A Scottish **Ghillie** *enters, singing a Gaelic song.*
He is followed by a grouse-shooting party of **British**, **French**, **German**, *and* **American** *munitions manufacturers with a* **Swiss** *banker. The* **Men** *need shooting sticks and the* **American**, *a wheelchair and black spectacles. 'Dead birds' falling from the flies are effective. The shooting party have a snack during the scene; bits of chicken, champagne, served by the* **Ghillie** *from a picnic basket.*

Ghillie It's a beautiful day for a shoot, sir.

Germany Sehr schön – sehr schön.

Ghillie Shall we drive them into the guns now, your lordship?

Britain Do that for me, Ewan.

The **Ghillie** *shouts Gaelic names and abuse.*

Chivvy them along now, Ewan.

Ghillie Coming over now, sir.

All shoot grouse and cry with delight, counting the birds they have shot.

France A wonderful year, Bertie.

Switzerland Highly successful.

Britain Yes, we still manage to fatten 'em up.

France   What were you saying about nickel, Von Possehl?

Germany   That last consignment – we didn't get it.

France   Well, we sent it.

Germany   Yes, well, you sent us some before, but I mean the latest consignment.

France   We sent it.

America   By which route?

France   Through Holland.

Britain   Aah, there's the fly in the ointment – Holland – very unreliable. The Scandinavian countries are much more convenient.

All (*to* **Germany**)   Bad luck – etc.

America   Hazards of war – loss of consignments.

Britain   Mind you, our navy's a bit to blame on that score, trying to set up a blockade of Germany.

America   You're telling me. We had three ships stopped by the British Navy last month.

Britain   Well, there you are – it's these unrealistic elements at work – they've just taken Jacks & Co. to court for exporting iron ore to Germany. They've got a blacklist, too – and I'm on it.

Germany   My Government want to shoot me.

America   You're on their shortlist!

Britain   Mind you, they'll never publish it – we bought out some of the papers, you know. Can't break up a union like ours in a few minutes.

Germany (*shoots*)   Another one for me.

Britain   That's a duck, not a grouse.

Germany   Well, I shoot anything.

Britain   So I've noticed. We'll export it to you for fat via Denmark.

Germany   When are you going to export some shillings for the Krupps fuses you are using in your English grenades?

Britain   All in good time, all in good time . . .

Switzerland   Swiss banks are always open, except in the lunch hour.

America   Very funny. Look, do you stumblebums realize that there have been two peace scares in the last year? Our shares dropped forty per cent.

France   What have your exports to Europe in the last three years amounted to? Ten and a half billion dollars.

America   Yeah, but all we're getting paid in now is your beautifully engraved paper money. That's what we're worried about.

Switzerland   What are you going to do with all that paper money if the Germans win?

Britain   It's no use being the biggest creditor in the world if no-one can pay you.

America   If the U.S. enters the war, that might just finish it.

Germany   Now, now, that's very dangerous talk.

Britain   I say, no need to lose your rag.

America   All right, all right, so long as peace doesn't break out. What about that peace scare in France, Count? Caused a flutter on Wall Street, I can tell you. Have you scotched it?

France   We flooded our papers with talk of defeatism and shot every pacifist we could find.

America   Good. I've a cheque for sixty million dollars in my pocket. I want to be able to cash it.

Switzerland   Who is it from?

America   Russia.

Switzerland   You'll never be able to cash it.

Germany   Don't spoil a beautiful day. I have interests in Russia.

Ghillie   How do you think the war's progressing, sir?

Britain   Oh, not too badly – everything's under control.

Ghillie   Do you think we'll have peace by Christmas?

America   Peace?

Germany   Peace? Where did he get that story?

France   War to the finish.

Switzerland   You must understand, my dear fellow, that war is a political and economic necessity.

Ghillie   Yes, sir, we've six of the family at the front, sir.

Britain   Keeps 'em off the streets.

Ghillie   That's what my mother says, sir. She's very proud of them, and the allowance helps her and me quite a bit.

America   Makes men of them.

France   There will always be a problem of surplus population.

America   I'm very glad you have due respect for your mother. I'll have you know, keeper, my President is deeply grieved by this war and you can tell your mother this – he regards the whole thing as a tragedy.

Britain   I understand he's a very sick man.

America   Yes, he's an idealist.

They all drink rapid toasts.

President Wilson!

France   Président Poincaré!

Britain   The King!

Germany   The Kaiser!

America   He's one of your shareholders, isn't he?

France   La belle France – our published profit last year was eight million sterling.

They all congratulate him.

Britain   Well done – new springs of wealth arise from war – as the saying goes.

America   It advances scientific discovery.

France   War is the life blood of a nation.

Germany   Well, I wish you'd tell my Government that; they want to shoot me.

All   No, why?

Germany   You tell me. My wife, she wore her eyes out, rolling bandages for the boys. I had to buy her spectacles. She never had bad eyes before. Fifty thousand marks I gave to the widows' and orphans' fund.

All   What's the trouble, old chap – why do they want to shoot you?

Germany   It's my Russian munitions factory.

Britain   Oh yes, how are they doing?

Germany   Twenty-four hour shifts. They're turning out bombs and shells all the time.

All   Good, well done – etc.

Germany   I'm a patriot, but I'm also a businessman; my stock-holders must have dividends. If I didn't make the profits, the Russians would. The people who ought to be shot are those who break international agreements. Germany and France agreed not to bombard the iron-ore works at Briey and Thionville for the duration – and some idiot pilot bombs them. A Frenchman.

America What happened to him?

France He was court-martialled.

Germany Good.

America A hero – eh?

Britain (*finds this very funny*) Rather a shock to be court-martialled, isn't it? Nobody asked questions?

France Oh yes – we had delegations, protests – I dealt with them – a hush has fallen. (**All**: *Bravo!*)

America You're smart, Count – you know he got a consignment of barbed wire from Germany through for Verdun only two months before the battle. Isn't that right, Comte?

Britain You mean the German chappies were caught on their own barbed wire? I say that's a bit near the knuckle, what! Dashed clever, though.

Switzerland We must take some credit for that.

Britain Yes, ten per cent, no doubt.

America Talking of credit. I promised the guys back home – and I hope you'll meet them some day – to pass on some of their handouts. (*Hands a card.*) Bethlehem Steel – furnish arms to every quarter of the globe. Cleveland Automatic Machine Company. (*Offers one to* **Switzerland**.)

Switzerland Not for me, we're neutral.

America It's a recipe for hot chocolate. (*To* **Britain**.) Hermann Rapide, fires non-stop for fifty hours – we tried to sell these things to the Germans before the war, but they turned us down. Serve 'em right if they lose the war.

Germany Ah, the shrapnel-making machine – you use acids to kill men?

Britain Four hours it takes, very effective.

Germany You have some pretty good chemists in America, of German extraction, no doubt.

Britain If it's all the same to you, old boy, we'll stick to the dear old Enfield rifles, cheap and easy to make.

Germany (*looking at pamphlet*) No gas? Ah yes – der grausame stille Tod.

America Deadly silent death.

Germany We use phosgene – cylinders 1.4 metres long, highly portable in the trenches – go on a man's back – he can carry a rifle as well.

America Look at our arsenal at Edgeworth, Maryland. We've developed sixty-three different poison gases and we've got eight more ready.

Britain Well, the old chlorine's pretty good. Haig's trying it out this moment at Loos. Mind you, we haven't heard from him. Yet.

All off except the **American**, *who remains in his wheelchair. Voices offstage sing 'Gassed Last Night' as a sequence of slides appear on the screen. The* **American** *goes off during the song.*

Slide 22: Infantry advancing along the crest of a hill, silhouetted against a large white cloud.

Slide 23: Two German infantrymen running to escape an advancing cloud of poison gas.

Slide 24: A group of 'walking wounded' Tommies, some with bandaged eyes owing to being gassed.

Slide 25: Group of four German soldiers, carrying one of their gassed in a blanket.

Slide 26: Line-up, Indian file, of gassed Tommies, all with bandaged eyes, and one hand on the shoulder of the person immediately in front of them.

Slide 27: Another picture of 'walking wounded': two French Poilus, eyes bandaged, walking hand in hand, escorted by another Frenchman and a Tommy.

Slide 28: Photograph of a German infantryman diving for cover, beside a field gun, as a shell explodes nearby.

Slide 29: Three British infantrymen, full pack, standing in mud and slush, firing over the parapet of a trench.

Slide 30: Three Germans in a dugout, silhouetted against clouds of

smoke caused by a plane bombing overhead.
Slide 31: Four Tommies sitting in dugouts, which are merely holes,
waist deep in mud.
Slide 32: A dead German soldier, lying in a slit trench.

Song   GASSED LAST NIGHT

[22] Gassed last night and gassed the night before, [23]
Going to get gassed tonight if we never get gassed any
   more. [24]
When we're gassed we're sick as we can be,
'Cos phosgene [25] and mustard gas is much too much
   for me.
They're warning [26] us, they're warning us,
One [27] respirator for the four of us.
Thank your lucky stars that three of us can run,
So one of us can use it all alone. [29]

Bombed last night and bombed the night before,
Going to get bombed tonight if we never get bombed
   any more.
When we're bombed we're [29] scared as we can be.
God strafe the bombing planes from High Germany.

They're [30] over us, they're over us,
One shell hole for just the [31] four of us,
Thank your lucky stars there are no more of us,
'Cos [32] one of us could fill it all alone.

A group of five **British Soldiers** *enter and build a barricade with*
the cones.

Sergeant   Get this barricade up, quickly. Keep your
heads down.

Lieutenant   Have you got the trench consolidated,
sergeant?

Sergeant   All present and correct, sir.

Lieutenant   The C.O. is going to have a word with the
men.

Sergeant   Right, lads – attention!

The **Commanding Officer** *enters.*

Commanding Officer   You can stand the men at ease, sergeant.

Sound of machine-gun fire. They throw themselves down.

Lieutenant   On your feet, lads.

Sergeant   Come on – jump to it!

Commanding Officer   You can let them smoke if they want to.

Sergeant   The C.O. says you can smoke. But don't let me catch you.

Commanding Officer   Now, you men, I've just come from having a powwow with the colonel; we think you've done some damn fine work – we congratulate you.

Soldiers   Thank you, sir.

Commanding Officer   I know you've had it pretty hard the last few days, bombs, shells, and snipers; we haven't escaped scot-free at staff either, I can tell you. Anyway, we're all here – well, not all of us, of course; and that gas of ours was pretty nasty – damned wind changing.

Lieutenant   Indeed, sir.

Commanding Officer   But these mishaps do happen in war, and gas can be a war-winning weapon. Anyway, so long as we can all keep smiling; you're white men all. (*To the* **Lieutenant**.) Sector all tidy now, Lieutenant?

Lieutenant   Well, we've buried most of the second Yorks and Lancs, sir; there's a few D.L.I.s and the men from our own company left.

Commanding Officer   I see. Well, look, let the lads drum up some char . . .

Sound of exploding shell.

Lieutenant   Get down, sir.

Commanding Officer   Good God!

Voice (*offstage*)   Stretcher bearers! ... Stretcher bearers! ...

Commanding Officer   You have no stretcher bearers over there?

Lieutenant   No, I'm afraid they went in the last attack, sir. I'm waiting for reliefs from H.Q.

Commanding Officer   Oh well, they're stout chaps!

Explosion.

Commanding Officer   Yes, you'd better let the men keep under cover.

Lieutenant   Thank you, sir.

Commanding Officer   Damn place still reeks of decomposing bodies.

Lieutenant   I'm afraid it's unavoidable, sir; the trench was mainly full of Jerries.

Commanding Officer   Yes, of course, you were more or less sharing the same front line for a couple of days, weren't you?

Lieutenant   Yes, sir.

Commanding Officer   Oh well, carry on.

Lieutenant   Thank you, sir.

Commanding Officer   Ye Gods! What's that?

Lieutenant   Oh, it's a Jerry, sir.

Commanding Officer   What?

Lieutenant   It's a leg, sir.

Commanding Officer   Well, get rid of it, man. You can't have an obstruction sticking out of the parapet like that.

He goes off.

Lieutenant   Hardcastle. Remove the offending limb.

Sergeant   Well, we can't do that, sir; it's holding up the parapet. We've just consolidated the position.

Lieutenant   Well, get a shovel and hack it off; and then dismiss the men.

He goes off.

Sergeant   Right, sir. (*Aside.*) An' what the bloody 'ell will I hang my equipment on. All right, lads, get back, get yourselves some char. Heads, trunks, blood all over the place, and all he's worried about is a damned leg.

The **Soldiers** *go off.*

Newspanel   EASTER 1916 . . . REBELLION IN IRELAND.

Band   INTRO. TO ROSES OF PICARDY

A figure dressed in black enters, holding on his head a plant pot spouting pampas grass. He takes his place right of centre. An elegant lady and her partner enter and stand on either side of him. They sing 'Roses of Picardy' with simple sincerity.

Song   ROSES OF PICARDY

Roses are shining in Picardy in the hush of the silver
   dew.
Roses are flowering in Picardy but there's never a rose
   like you.
And the roses will die with the summertime and our
   roads may be far, far apart
But there's one rose that dies not in Picardy. 'Tis the
   rose that I keep in my heart.

Band   WALTZ: LONG, LONG TRAIL

The characters dance on in couples up left, circling round **Plant Pot***, timing their dialogue to be heard as they dance past him, downstage.*
They are **Sir John French** *and partner,* **Sir William Robertson** *and partner,* **Sir Douglas Haig** *and* **Lady Haig***. The couple who sang 'Roses of Picardy' join them, becoming*

the **First Officer** *and his* **Partner**. *Another army officer, dancing on with a partner, is the* **Second Officer**. *During the dance* **Rawlinson** *wanders in and stands looking on in a suitable pose.*

The ladies wear tiaras or feathers as head-dress and have long, light drapes of soft colours or white.

The scene should be played elegantly, using the upper-class accents of the period. The use of 'what' at the end of a sentence is not a question, merely an affectation of the period.
Apart from **Lady Haig**, *the actresses use their own names, with appropriate titles.*

Plant Pot   Sir John French, Commander-in-Chief of His Majesty's Forces, Miss Fanny Carby.

Fanny   Isn't that Sir Douglas Haig – the new man?

French   Yes. Damned upstart. That other blighter Robertson's here, too.

Fanny   Intrigue upon intrigue.

French   Hold your tongue, Fanny.

Plant Pot   Sir William Robertson, The Honourable Ann Beach.

Ann   I was so thrilled to hear of your new appointment, Willy.

Robertson   One takes these things as they come, you know, Annie.

Ann   Sir Henry Wilson's green with envy.

Robertson   Quite.

Ann   He's just behind us, dancing with that frump, Lady Myvanwy.

Plant Pot   Sir Henry Wilson, The Lady Myvanwy Jenn.

Wilson   The mess was vastly relieved when they changed their name from Wettin to Windsor.

Myvanwy   They're still Germans, Sir Henry.

Wilson   But it's very unpatriotic to say so, Lady Myvanwy.

Plant Pot   Sir Douglas and Lady Haig.

Haig   Canter in the row tomorrow before breakfast, Doris?

Lady Haig   Don't forget your fitting, Douglas, the new boots.

Haig   And we're lunching at No. 10 – without French.

Lady Haig   Congratulations, my dear.

Myvanwy   What on earth do they see in him?

Wilson   Shoots pheasant with the Prince of Wales. Lady Doris was one of Queen Alexandra's maids of honour.

Myvanwy   Really ... What!

Wilson   So now he has the ear of the King, of course.

Fanny   Haig! Sir Douglas Haig! The name rings a bell.

French   Whisky.

Fanny (*stops in her tracks*)   Trade!

French   'Fraid so.

The dance ends with a swirl. The **Men** *get together in clumps and guffaw over dirty jokes. The* **Women** *talk in groups.*

Robertson   Toby Rawlinson!

Rawlinson   You have the better of me.

Robertson   Karachi!

Rawlinson   Polo ponies!

Robertson   Do excuse me.

Rawlinson   Certainly.

Ann   Well, I've volunteered for the V.A.D.

Myvanwy   Really ... What!

Ann   The uniform is so becoming.

Sir John French *turns towards* **Robertson**, *who arrives back with a drink.*

Robertson   Haven't had an opportunity to talk, sir, since my appointment was announced, but I'd like to say how proud I am to serve under you ...

French *turns his back on him. Hushed reaction.*

French (*mutters*)   Like to talk to my officers without interruption sometimes.

Rawlinson   Rather, what!

Robertson   May I take you home, Annie?

Ann *pulls a face.*

Rawlinson   Good night, Sir John. Ball's in your court, Wilson.

First Lady (*the singer*)   What was all that about?

Fanny   Sir John thinks Sir Henry is the perfect man for the job.

First Lady   Sir Henry Wilson?

Myvanwy (*aside to* **Lady Haig**)   Keeps him waiting like a lackey.

French   A word in your private ear, Wilson.

Wilson   Yes, sir.

French   Now do take that sour expression off your face.

Wilson   I've always understood from you, sir, that the job was mine.

French   Well, it's your own fault. You're such a brute. You'll never be nice to people you don't like. Anyhow, the day's by no means lost. You'll have to make love to Asquith when you meet him.

Wilson I'm too suspicious of Kitchener and Churchill to make love to anyone – anyway Asquith hates me – none of them are friends of yours either; you know that, of course.

French Oh yes, quite. Anyway, I'm showing them the sort of man I am. Giving Robertson the position I marked down for you. I've refused to mess with him – pretty good, what! Snubbing him just now in the middle of the room.

Wilson You made your attitude pretty clear, sir.

French Well, there you are then. You depend on me. I'm very fond of you, Henry.

Wilson Thank you, sir.

French So keep your pecker up and don't be so gloomy.

Myvanwy (*to* **Wilson**) I wouldn't trust him an inch.

Wilson I don't.

Lady Haig (*to the* **First Officer**, *the singer*) I will tell you in confidence, my dear, His Majesty very much hopes that my husband will succeed French.

First Officer My God!

Lady Haig Yes, oh yes, Douglas thinks French is quite unfitted for the high position he's been called to.

Second Officer (*turning to* **Haig**, *sotto voce*) Who was Sir John's little . . . lady friend?

Haig Rank outsider.

Second Officer I quite believe it.

Haig It's a flaw in his character, you know, his weakness for the fair sex. Loses all sense of decency.

Second Officer Really, sir!

Haig Yes, well, he had to borrow two thousand pounds from me at Aldershot over a woman.

Second Officer Good God, sir!

Haig   And he was Commander of my Cavalry brigade at the time.

Second Officer   Damn bad show, sir, borrowing from a subordinate.

Haig   Appalling!

Band   A MERE WHISPER OF COMRADES

French   Haig!

Haig   Sir John!

They advance and shake hands. Applause.

French   You saw me snub Robertson just now?

Haig   I did, Sir John.

French   That's the way to treat 'em.

A **Photographer** *comes in and takes a picture.*

'Friends in sunshine and shadow' – put that in your photogravure, boy.

Photographer   The right man in the right job, if I may say so, sir.

French   You may, you may. Thank you, my man. Well, how did you leave the men at the front, Douglas?

Haig   Oh, in fine heart, sir, just spoiling for a fight.

French   Makes one feel very proud. A word in your private ear, Douglas. What do you think of that man Kitchener?

Haig   Well, sir –

French   The man's intolerable. He's behaving like a Generalissimo now – he's only a damned politician.

Haig   With regard to that, sir. You know he turned up in Paris in his uniform again.

French   My God, no! He's no damned right to a uniform at all – I mean Secretary of State for War – what happened?

Haig   Well, it raised some pretty tricky points of protocol.

French   Yes, well – what are we going to do about it?

Band   WALTZ: APREZ LA GUERRE

Fanny   Johnnie.

French   Excuse me. They're playing my tune. That man Kitchener is more of an enemy to the B.E.F. than Moltke or Ludendorff.

The couples begin waltzing again and gradually go off.

Myvanwy   How did that man Haig get his pips, if you tell me he failed all his staff college entrance examinations?

Wilson   Duke of Cambridge.

Myvanwy   What?

Wilson   Friend of the family.

Myvanwy   Oh! yes, on her side.

Wilson   Waived the formalities and let him in.

French   Yes, well, he may have lent me £2,000, but he made a terrible mess of his field exercises.

Second Officer (*to* **Haig**)   Good night, sir.

First Officer *and* **Lady** (*to* **Haig**)   Good night.

Haig (*doesn't answer*)   That man is a terrible intriguer.

Lady Haig   Yes, I can tell by his deceitful face.

Haig   And he's flabby!

Lady Haig   You've been loyal long enough, my dear.

Haig   Well, No. 10 tomorrow, Doris.

Lady Haig   And a field-marshal's job for you.

Voices Offstage   My carriage!
Carriages!

Good night!

Men's *voices offstage sing 'Hush, here comes a Whizzbang' very softly: a sequence of slides is projected as follows:*

Slide 33: Night photographs of flares, and various Very lights.
Slide 34: Photograph of a cloud formation.
Slide 35: Three Tommies walking across duckboards in a muddy field.
Slide 36: Dead Germans lying in a shallow trench in a peaceful-looking country field.
Slide 37: A young French soldier, obviously on burial duty, laden with wooden crosses.
Slide 38: Dead French Poilus; one of them has a smile on his face.
Slide 39: A field with nothing but white wooden crosses as far as one can see.

Song   HUSH, HERE COMES A WHIZZBANG

(*Tune: 'Hush, here comes the Dream Man'*)

[33] Hush, here comes a whizzbang, [34]
Hush, here comes a whizzbang, [35]
Now, you soldier men, get down those stairs, [36]
Down in your dugouts and say your prayers. [37]
Hush, here comes a whizzbang,
And it's making [38] straight for you,
And you'll see all the wonders [39] of no man's land,
If a whizzbang hits you.

Haig (*entering*)   Germany has shot her bolt. The prospects for 1916 are excellent.

British General (*entering*)   Permission to speak, sir.

Haig   Of course.

Slide 40: A map of Ypres and the surrounding district, showing Kitchener's Wood, Hill 60, Passchendaele, etc.

British General   If we continue in this way, the line of trenches will stretch from Switzerland to the sea. Neither we nor the Germans will be able to break through. The war will end in complete stalemate.

Haig   Nonsense. We need only one more big offensive to break through and win. My troops are of fine quality, and specially trained for this type of war.

British General   This is not war, sir, it is slaughter.

Haig   God is with us. It is for King and Empire.

British General   We are sacrificing lives at the rate of five to sometimes fifty thousand a day.

Haig   One battle, our superior morale, bombardment.

Junior Officer (*entering*)   Sir, tell us what to do and we'll do it.

Haig   We're going to walk through the enemy lines.

British General *and* **Junior Officer** *go off.*

Slide 40 fades into Slide 41: Tommies advancing across no man's land, in full battle pack, silhouetted against clouds.

A man's voice, offstage, sings slowly as **Haig** *speaks.*

Song   THERE'S A LONG, LONG TRAIL

There's a long, long trail a-winding
Into the land of my dreams,
Where the nightingale is singing
And the white moon beams . . .

He carries on humming the tune, ending:

. . . till the day when I'll be going down that long, long
trail with you.

Haig (*during the song*)   Complete victory . . . the destruction of German militarism . . . victory march on Berlin . . . slow deliberate fire is being maintained on the enemy positions . . . at this moment my men are advancing across no man's land in full pack, dressing from left to right; the men are forbidden under pain of court-martial to take cover in any shell hole or dugout . . . their magnificent morale will cause the enemy to flee in confusion . . . the attack will be driven home with the bayonet . . . I feel that every step I take is guided by the divine will.

Sounds of heavy bombardment.

Newspanel   FEBRUARY ... VERDUN ... TOTAL LOSS ONE
AND A HALF MILLION MEN.

Haig (*looking through field-glasses*)   This is most unsatisfactory.
Where are the Sherwood Foresters? Where are the East
Lancs on the right?

British General (*who has entered during above speech*)   Out in
no man's land.

Haig   They are sluggish from too much sitting in the
trenches.

British General   Most of them, sir, will never rise again.

Haig   We must break through.

British General   Regardless of loss, sir?

Haig   The loss of, say, another 300,000 men may lead to
really great results.

British General   Yes, sir.

Haig   And will not impede our ability to continue the
offensive. In any case, we have to calculate on another
great offensive next year.

British General   If the slackers on the Home Front see
it our way, sir.

Haig   Quite.

British General   We are rather short of men, sir.

Haig   What's left?

British General   The new chappies from Ireland have
just arrived.

Haig   Rather wild untrained lot! Still, they'll be raring to
have a crack at the Boche, and what they lack in training,
they'll make up for in gallantry.

British General   They've just got off the train. Most of them haven't eaten for forty-eight hours –

Haig   They are moving against a weakened and demoralised enemy. Capture the German line, without further delay.

Three **Irish Soldiers***, one of them a* **Sergeant***, enter. They wear English army caps and, over their Pierrot costumes, plain green kilts. The* **First Soldier** *carries a Union Jack on a pole. They must be good dancers.*

Sergeant   Right boys, up and at 'em!

First *and* **Second Soldier**   Up the Irish!

Band   IRISH WASHERWOMAN

All three dance an advance based on the jig, 'The Irish Washerwoman' played on the pipes. The flag is carried high. Bombardment. They fling themselves down, having reached their goal. The bagpipes fade. Birdsong.

Sergeant   We made it.

First Soldier   Where are we, Serg?

Sergeant   I reckon we've broken into a lull.

Second Soldier   Lovely, is it not? Peaceful.

First Soldier   Peaceful? An' what's that dirty great mound of earth confrontin' us?

Sergeant   Isn't it an earthwork then? An' near enough to protect us.

Sniper's bullet.

First Soldier   What was that?

Sergeant   Must have been a stray one. All the same, keep your heads down, fellers. You see, the trouble is, we've been fightin' too well. We've arrived ahead of ourselves.

First Soldier   How many trenches did we capture, Serg?

Sergeant   About nine, I reckon.

Second Soldier   Ten.

Sergeant   Make it a round dozen an' we'll be mentioned in dispatches!

Second Soldier   We'll be heroes.

First Soldier   'Twill be one up for the Irish Fusiliers!

Distant birdsong.

Second Soldier   What was that, Serg?

Sergeant   What was what?

Second Soldier   Sounded like someone callin'.

Sergeant   Where?

Second Soldier   Beyond the mound.

First Soldier   It'll be Limey wounded. A lot fell in that last attack . . . in that shell hole over there.

Second Soldier   There it is again.

They all listen.

Sergeant (*repeating what he hears*)   'Come back. Come back, you bloody fools.'

Second Soldier   He's telling us to go back?

Sergeant (*calls*)   T'anks, mush! Get that flag down!

First Soldier   Get back thro' all that? Easier said than done.

Sergeant   Shut up. (*He listens.*) He says we're drawin' their fire.

Sniper's bullet.

First Soldier   Where did that come from?

Sergeant   Bejasus, that was one of ours.

Second Soldier (*shouts*)   Don't shoot, it's us. There's human beings over here!

Heavy gunfire. They flatten themselves.

Sergeant   Now see what you've done, you bloody eejit! Seamus!

First Soldier   Serg?

Sergeant   You're quick on your pins. Get back to H.Q.! Pronto! Tell the artillery to raise their bloody sights a bit an' –

First Soldier   Back through all that?

Sergeant   – save their shells for Jerry.

First Soldier   On me own?

Sergeant   It's hard to give ground now we've got so near our goal.

First Soldier   I see that. You want me to tell 'em we've won.

Sergeant   Do that!

First Soldier   The battle's won.

And tentatively he makes his way upstage and stops.

First Soldier (*calls quietly*)   Hey, Serg! That last one got the bridge.

Second Soldier   That means we're cut off.

Sergeant (*calls quietly*)   Give yourself a treat! Swim for it. (*The* **Sergeant** *and the* **Second Soldier** *watch, listen.*) That'll be the first bath he's had this year. (*He watches, then whistles.*) Seamus! Bring us back a bottle of whiskey . . . Irish.

Sniper's bullet.

Second Soldier   He's gone under, Serg.

Sergeant (*crosses himself*)   Yeah, they got him. (*He looks at the* **Second Soldier**.) Well, someone's got to go.

Second Soldier   Sure.

Sergeant   Seamus is gone. (*A pause.*) They'll think there's hundreds of us here.

Second Soldier   I could sprint that half a mile back in no time.

Sergeant   Get yourself a medal! (*The* **Second Soldier** *leaps up and away. Sniper's bullet.*) Well if he's got shot, I'll kill him. (*Heavy gunfire.*) There they go! That's the bloody mad English, shelling for the next attack. (*Heavy gunfire and explosion.*) Don't shoot, it's us! Stop firing! (*Sniper's bullet. The* **Sergeant** *slowly twists round, wounded. He puts his hands up.*) Kamerad! Kamerad! (*A strain of 'The Irish Washerwoman' is reprised faintly and slowly as, turning and turning, the* **Sergeant** *moves towards darkness. As he goes.*) It's not so bad. After all, I'll escape the whole bloomin' war.

The **M.C.** *comes on and sets a speaker's stand for* **Mrs Pankhurst**. *During the scene he stands at the edge of the crowd, a silent observer.* **Mrs Pankhurst** *enters, followed by a straggling crowd. As she steps up on to the stand one or two of the* **Men** *whistle.*

Mrs Pankhurst   Now before talking to you all, I should like to read you a letter from my friend George Bernard Shaw.

First Man (*shouts*)   Who's 'e when 'e's at 'ome?

Mrs Pankhurst   He says, 'The men of this country are being sacrificed to the blunders of boobies, the cupidity of capitalists –

First Woman (*aside*)   What's she talking abaht?

Mrs Pankhurst   '– the ambition of conquerors, the lusts and lies –

Second Woman (*on the word 'lusts'*)   Oo-er!

Mrs Pankhurst   '– and rancours of bloodthirsty men who love war because it opens their prison doors and sets them on the throne of power and popularity.'

Second Man (*shouts*)   Now give us a song!

Mrs Pankhurst   For the second time, peace is being offered to the sorely tried people of the civilised world –

Someone blows a raspberry.

Mrs Pankhurst   At the close of 1915 President Wilson proposed an immediate armistice to be followed by a peace conference.

Third Man   Watch it!

Mrs Pankhurst   In April of this year, Germany herself proposed peace.

Third Man (*louder*)   I said watch it!

Mrs Pankhurst   The peace movements are strong in England, France and the United States *and* in Germany even.

Men *and* **Women** (*together*)   That's enough! Leave it out! That'll do!

Mrs Pankhurst   In the Reichstag –

First Man   Who's 'e when 'e's at 'ome?

Mrs Pankhurst   – the peace groups are active and outspoken; the exact terms of Germany's offer have never been made known to us and I should like to ask Lloyd George what his aims are –

First Woman   An' I should like to arst you wot your ole man's gettin' for 'is dinner.

Mrs Pankhurst   The politicians chatter like imbeciles while civilisation bleeds to death.

Third Man   Treason! That's treason!

Second Man   That's right.

Mrs Pankhurst   I should like to ask that gentleman if –

Second Man   Don't ask me, love. I'm iggerant!

First Man   S'right! 'E don't know nuffink.

Mrs Pankhurst   I would ask him to consider the plight of the civilised world after one more year! Do you know what you do? No! And the statesmen wash their hands of the whole affair.

First Woman   Why don't you wash your face?

Third Man   'Aig's got 'em on the run! 'Aig!

Mrs Pankhurst   Who tells you this? *The Times*?

Second Man   'E's right. 'Aig's the boy.

Mrs Pankhurst   The newspaper that refuses to publish the pacifist letters, that distorts the truth about our so-called victories? Slowly but surely, we are killing off the finest and best of the male population!

First Woman (*shouting*)   'Ere, don't you address them words to me!

Second Woman   No! Don't you address them words to 'er!

Mrs Pankhurst   The sons of Europe are being crucified –

First Woman   My ole man's at the front –

Second Woman   She's 'ad 'er share of suffering!

Mrs Pankhurst   – crucified on the barbed wire, because you, the misguided masses still cry for war.

Second Woman   Yeah! Kill 'em all!

First Woman   Down with the 'Un!

Mrs Pankhurst   War cannot be won!

Cries and boos, 'Shut yer face!', 'Or we'll shut it for you!'

Mrs Pankhurst (*struggling to be heard*)   No-one can win a war!

The cries mount.

Mrs Pankhurst   Do you want the war to go on till

Germany is beaten to the ground?

Newspanel   JULY 1 ... SOMME ... BRITISH LOSS 60,000 MEN ON THE FIRST DAY.

A roar of approval which melts into singing.

Crowd   Rule Britannia! Britannia rules the waves, Britons, never, never, never, shall be slaves.

Two **Drunken Soldiers** *come on as the crowd disperses and, without over-acting, sing.*

Song   I DON'T WANT TO BE A SOLDIER

(*Tune: 'I'll make a man of you'*)

I don't want to be a soldier,
I don't want to go to war,
I'd rather stay at home,
Around the streets to roam,
And live on the earnings of a lady typist.
I don't want a bayonet in my belly,
I don't want my bollocks shot away,
I'd rather stay in England,
In merry, merry England,
And fornicate my bleeding life away.

The other **Soldiers** *run on.*

Haig (*entering*)   Attack on the Somme!

M.C.   Right dress! Eyes front! Left turn! We're going along the line.

Sergeant   Quick march!

The **Men** *march round the stage whistling 'Pop Goes the Weasel'. They end up kneeling in line behind* **Haig**.

Haig   We shall launch a decisive attack which will carry us through the German lines. We shall advance on Belgium to the Channel Ports. The people at home have given us the means to mass every man, horse, and gun on the Western Front. It is our duty to attack the enemy until his last resources are exhausted and his line breaks. Then in will go our cavalry and annihilate him. I am the predestined instrument of providence for the achievement of victory for the British Army.

Two **Englishwomen** *enter on either side of the stage and shout across to one another.*

First Englishwoman   Hey, Bett!

Second Englishwoman   Yeah? What?

First Englishwoman   You know what they're doing now?

Second Englishwoman   No, what?

First Englishwoman   Melting corpses for glycerine.

Second Englishwoman   Get away! Who?

First Englishwoman   The Germans. It's in this morning's paper.

Two **German Women** *enter on the balconies, left and right, and shout to one another.*

First German Woman   Emma! Emma!

Second German Woman   Ja?

First German Woman   Weisst du, was sie jetzt tun?

Second German Woman   Nein, was?

First German Woman   Sie schmelzen Körper für Glyzerin.

Second German Woman   Wirklich! Wer?

First German Woman   Die Engländer. Es war in der Zeitung heute Morgen.

First Englishwoman   Bett – do you want to know something else? They say there's another big push coming.

Second Englishwoman   Oh God.

First German Woman (*during preceding two speeches*)   Emma! Man sagt noch ein Angriff kommt.

Second German Woman   Sagst du? Mein Gott.

The four **Women** *go off.*

Haig   Advance!

The **Soldiers** *rise and march round singing.*

Song   KAISER BILL

(Tune: 'Pop goes the Weasel')

Kaiser Bill is feeling ill,
The Crown Prince, he's gone barmy.
We don't give a cluck for old von Fluck
And all his bleeding army.

Australian Voice *(distant, high up in the auditorium)*   Are you
the reinforcements?

Sergeant   Yeah! On our way up to Vimy.

Voice   Wouldn't go up there if I were you; they've got a
shortage!

One of the Soldiers   What of? Ammunition?

Voice   No. Coffins!

Sergeant   Right, lads. Form fours. Rum ration.

The **Men** *kneel again.*

Haig   It's now or never.

British General   Runners!

The **Men** *are centre stage and sing, marking time. Two* **Runners**
set up tables with field telephones at opposite sides of the stage. **Haig**
and the **British General** *sit talking into the phones and two*
Runners *cross backwards and forwards taking messages.*

Song   THEY WERE ONLY PLAYING LEAPFROG

(Tune: 'John Brown's Body')

One staff officer jumped right over another staff officer's
    back.
And another staff officer jumped right over that other

staff officer's back,
A third staff officer jumped right over two other staff
officers' backs,
And a fourth staff officer jumped right over all the other
staff officers' backs.

They were only playing leapfrog,
They were only playing leapfrog,
They were only playing leapfrog,
When one staff officer jumped right over another staff
officer's back.

The song is sung a second time quietly under **Haig** *and the*
British General, *who are talking simultaneously.*

Haig   Hello. G.O.C.-in-C. Clear the line, please. Look, I
must have the Eighth Division forward on the right ... Yes
I must have Eighth Division ... I see, seventy per cent
casualties ... I must have Eighth Division forward on the
right wing ... (*The following sentence heard clearly.*) No, you
must reserve the artillery; we are using too many shells.

British General   Are you ready there? We are ready
here ... Have receipted your orders to advance ... Are
you ready there? ... We are ready here ... Are you ready
there? ... We are ready here ... and approved.... (*The
following sentence heard clearly.*) Night has fallen. The clouds are
gathering. The men are lost somewhere in no man's land.

Runner   Seventy per cent casualties, sir.

British General   Then there is a corner of some foreign
land that is forever England.

Haig   We shall attack at dawn!

Sergeant   Right. Dig in for the night, lads. Pack off.

Haig *and the* **British General** *continue working at their tables.*
The **Soldiers** *remove their kit and settle down for the night.*

First Soldier (*sings*)   Old soldiers never die,
   The young ones wish they would.

Second Soldier   Can you hear those poor wounded

bleeders moaning in no man's land?

Third Soldier   Sounds like a cattle market.

Haig   Attack at five ack emma.

British General   Attack, five ack emma.

The two **Runners** *sleep, standing up. The* **Soldiers** *sing softly.*

Song   IF YOU WANT THE OLD BATTALION

If you want the old battalion,
We know where they are, we know where they are,
We know where they are,
If you want the old battalion, we know where they are,
They're hanging on the old barbed wire,
We've seen them, we've seen them,
Hanging on the old barbed wire,
We've seen them, we've seen them,
Hanging on the old barbed wire.

Haig   Monday, noon. Our offensive commenced this
morning; satisfactory progress. Monday evening. The
trouble was that the men waved their hats instead of flags
as His Majesty rode by. I tried the mare out the day
before. The King did clutch the reins too firmly . . .
correction . . . the King did clutch the reins rather firmly.
No reflection on His Majesty's horsemanship. The grass
was very slippery and the mare moved backwards; she was
upset. I'd exercised her every day for a year.

Song   FAR FAR FROM WIPERS

(*Tune: 'Sing me to sleep'*)

Far far from Wipers, I long to be,
Where German snipers can't get at me,
Damp is my dugout, cold are my feet,
Waiting for whizzbangs to put me to sleep.

A bugle sounds reveille.

Haig   So unfortunate it had to be my horse that threw
the King.

Reveille sounds again.

Haig's Runner   Five ack emma, sir.

Haig (*into the telephone*)   Press the attack immediately.

British General (*into the telephone*)   The losses were very heavy last night, sir. The Canadian corps had very heavy casualties . . .

He continues his report on losses. The **Soldiers** *begin to pick up their kit. One of them sings.*

Song   IF THE SERGEANT STEALS YOUR RUM

(*Tune: 'Never Mind'*)

If the sergeant steals your rum, never mind,
If the sergeant steals your rum, never mind;
Though he's just a blinking sot,
Let him have the bloody lot,
If the sergeant steals your rum, never mind.

British General (*continuing*)   . . . the 13th London were isolated and completely wiped out by their own cross-fire.

Haig   There must be no squeamishness over losses. Give orders to advance immediately.

The two **Officers** *retire upstage and watch.*

Sergeant   Right, over the top, boys.

Explosion. They charge and fling themselves on the ground. Machine-guns.

Jerry's doin' well.

First Soldier   What are all them little yellow flags out there?

Second Soldier   They give them to our blokes.

First Soldier   What for?

Second Soldier   So they'd know where we was.

Sergeant   Did you say our blokes?

Second Soldier   Yeah.

First Soldier   Oh, I get it, so our guns don't get us before Jerry does.

Explosion.

Sergeant   You stick with me, lads. I'll see you through this lot. Heads down and keep spread well out.

Second Soldier (*sings*)   Far far from Wipers I long to be.

Sergeant   Blimey! You still here?

Second Soldier   Yeah! Why?

Sergeant   I drew you in the sweep.

A shell explodes.

I've had enough of this.

Second Soldier   Me and all.

Sergeant   Every man for himself.

Third Soldier   Every man for himself.

Second Soldier   See you after the war, sarg.

Sergeant   Yeah, in the Red Lion.

First Soldier   Eight o'clock.

Sergeant   Make it half past.

First Soldier   Eh?

Sergeant   I might be a bit late.

The **Soldiers** *go off.*

British General   Permission to speak, sir? I have been wondering, or rather the staff and I have been wondering, perhaps this policy of attrition might be a mistake. After all, it's wearing us down more than it is them. Couldn't we try a policy of manoeuvre on other fronts?

Haig   Nonsense. The Western Front is the only real front. We must grind them down. You see, our population is greater than theirs and their losses are greater than ours.

British General I don't quite follow that, sir.

Haig In the end they will have five thousand men left and we will have ten thousand and we shall have won. In any case, I intend to launch one more full-scale offensive, and we shall break through and win.

Junior Officer (*entering*) I say, sir, did you know that the average life of a young subaltern at the front has now increased to three weeks.

Second Officer (*entering*) Yes, sir, and replacements are coming in by the thousand; it's marvellous. (*Exit.*)

Junior Officer It's an empire in arms. (*Exit.*)

Haig You see, the staff are in complete accord.

British General Yes, sir. And the morale of the civilian population has never been higher.

The murderer, **Landru***, enters, dragging the body of a* **Woman** *followed by a* **Gendarme***.*

Landru Excusez-moi, s'il vous plaît.

Gendarme Hey! M. Landru! Where are you going with that body?

Landru I am going to bury it. With all this killing going on and they never called me up, I thought I'd settle a few private scores.

Gendarme Good idea! . . . How many have you done?

Landru Twelve wives, so far.

Gendarme Hey! Just a minute. You're for the guillotine.

Both go off.

Newspanel NOVEMBER . . . SOMME BATTLE ENDS . . . TOTAL LOSS 1,332,000 MEN . . . GAIN NIL.

The band plays a few bars of 'Twelfth Street Rag'. Three couples dance wildly and continue as the **Soldier** *in uniform sings.*

Song   I WORE A TUNIC

(Tune: 'I wore a Tulip')

I wore a tunic, a dirty khaki tunic,
And you wore your civvy clothes,
We fought and bled at Loos, while you were on the
    booze,
The booze that no one here knows.
You were out with the wenches, while we were in the
    trenches,
Facing an angry foe,
Oh, you were a-slacking, while we were attacking
The Germans on the Menin Road.

The dancers go off. **Haig**, *a* **Chaplain**, *a* **Nurse** *and*
Soldiers *come on.*

Chaplain   Let us pray.

All sing. These soldiers' songs must be sung like hymns. The
Chaplain, **Haig**, *and the* **Nurse** *sing the correct words.*

Song   FORWARD JOE SOAP'S ARMY

(Tune: 'Onward Christian Soldiers')

Forward Joe Soap's army, marching without fear,
With our old commander, safely in the rear.
He boasts and skites from morn till night,
And thinks he's very brave,
But the men who really did the job are dead and in
    their grave.
Forward Joe Soap's army, marching without fear,
With our old commander, safely in the rear.
Amen.

Chaplain   Dearly beloved brethren, I am sure you will be
glad to hear the news from the Home Front. The
Archbishop of Canterbury has made it known that it is no
sin to labour for the war on the Sabbath. I am sure you
would like to know that the Chief Rabbi has absolved your
Jewish brethren from abstaining from pork in the trenches.
And likewise his Holiness the Pope has ruled that the

eating of flesh on a Friday is no longer a venial sin . . .

Soldier (*aside, thrown away*)   High time we had an Irish pope . . .

Chaplain   And in far-away Tibet, the Dalai Lama has placed his prayers at the disposal of the Allies. Now, brethren, tomorrow being Good Friday, we hope God will look kindly on our attack on Arras.

Men   Amen.

Sergeant   We will now sing from Hymns Ancient and Modern, number 358, 'Waft, Waft, ye winds, waft, waft ye'.

Song   FRED KARNO'S ARMY

(*Tune: 'The Church's One Foundation'*)

We are Fred Karno's army,
The Ragtime Infantry,
We cannot fight, we cannot shoot,
What bleeding use are we?
And when we get to Berlin,
The Kaiser he will say,
Hoch, hoch, mein Gott, what a bloody rotten lot,
Are the Ragtime infantry!
Amen.

Chaplain   Let us pray. O God, show thy face to us as thou didst with thy angel at Mons. The choir will now sing 'What a friend we have in Jesus' as we offer a silent prayer for Sir Douglas Haig for success in tomorrow's onset.

Song   WHEN THIS LOUSY WAR IS OVER

(*Tune: 'What a friend we have in Jesus'*)

When this lousy war is over,
No more soldiering for me,
When I get my civvy clothes on,
Oh, how happy I shall be!
No more church parades on Sunday,
No more putting in for leave,
I shall kiss the sergeant major,

How I'll miss him, how he'll grieve!
Amen.

Chaplain O Lord, now lettest thou thy servant depart in peace, according to thy word. Dismiss.

Corporal (*blowing a whistle*) Come on, you men, fall in.

The **Soldiers** *sing as they march off.*

Song WASH ME IN THE WATER

Whiter than the whitewash on the wall,
Whiter than the whitewash on the wall,
Oh, wash me in the water that you wash your dirty
    daughter in,
And I shall be whiter than the whitewash on the wall,
On the wall . . .

Chaplain Land of our birth, we pledge to thee, our love and toil in the years to be.

Haig Well, God, the prospects for a successful attack are now ideal. I place myself in thy hands.

Chaplain Into thy hands I commend my spirit.

Nurse The fields are full of tents, O Lord, all empty except for as yet unmade and naked iron bedsteads. Every ward has been cleared to make way for the wounded that will be arriving when the big push comes.

Haig I trust you will understand, Lord, that as a British gentleman I could not subordinate myself to the ambitions of a junior foreign commander, as the politicians suggested. It is for the prestige of my King and Empire, Lord.

Chaplain Teach us to rule ourselves alway, controlled and cleanly night and day.

Haig I ask thee for victory, Lord, before the Americans arrive.

Nurse The doctors say there will be enormous numbers of dead and wounded, God.

Chaplain   That we may bring if need arise, no maimed or worthless sacrifice.

Haig   Thus to grant us fair weather for tomorrow's attack, that we may drive the enemy into the sea.

Nurse   O. Lord, I beg you, do not let this dreadful war cause all the suffering that we have prepared for. I know you will answer my prayer.

Explosion. They go off.

A sequence of slides is shown as **Soldiers**' *voices sing offstage.*

Slide 42: A group of eight or nine Highland infantrymen, around a small camp fire.
Slide 43: Two captured wounded German infantrymen, both sitting, one nursing a badly wounded leg, the other sewing.
Slide 44: A lull in the fighting. A trench of Tommies 'at ease' – some smoking, others doing running repairs on their kit.
Slide 45: Three Tommies walking through a rain-soaked muddy field.
Slide 46: Two captured Germans between two Tommies. One of the Germans is being given a drink of water by one of the Tommies.
Slide 47: A group of Tommies, skylarking and obviously off-duty, with a damaged old horse-drawn coach, upon which they've chalked '10 Downing Street'.

Song   I WANT TO GO HOME

[42] I want to go home, [43] I want to go home, [44]
I don't want to go in the trenches no more,
Where whizzbangs and shrapnel they whistle and roar.
    [45]
Take me over the sea, [46] where the Alleymen can't get
    at me; [47]
Oh my, I don't want to die, I want to go home.

Newspanel   BY NOV 1916 . . . TWO AND A HALF MILLION
MEN KILLED ON WESTERN FRONT.

The screen goes up to reveal **Soldiers** *in gas capes doing burial squad duty in mime.* **Haig** *is on one of the balconies.*

Haig   I thank you, God; the attack is a great success.

Fighting has been severe, but that was to be expected.
There has been some delay along the Menin Road, but the
ground is thick with enemy dead. First reports from the
clearing station state that our casualties are only some sixty
thousand: mostly slight. The wounded are very cheery
indeed.

The **Soldiers** *sing as they work.*

Song . THE BELLS OF HELL

> The bells of hell go ting-a-ling-a-ling,
> For you but not for me,
> And the little devils how they sing-a-ling-a-ling,
> For you but not for me.
> Oh death, where is thy sting-a-ling-a-ling,
> Oh grave, thy victory?
> The bells of hell go ting-a-ling-a-ling
> For you but not for me.

Newspanel   APRIL 17 ... AISNE ... ALLIED LOSS 180,000
MEN ... GAIN NIL.

The **Soldiers** *sing again, more gaily.* **Haig** *conducts them, wearing
a Pierrot hat, as they dance.*

> The bells of hell go ting-a-ling-a-ling,
> For you but not for me,
> And the little devils how they sing-a-ling-a-ling,
> For you but not for me.
> Oh death, where is thy sting-a-ling-a-ling,
> Oh grave, thy victory?
> The bells of hell go ting-a-ling-a-ling
> For you but not for me.

A **Medical Officer** *and a* **Nurse** *enter.*

Medical Officer   We'll have to start burning them soon,
nurse, instead of burying them.

Nurse   Yes, it's such an unpleasant duty, doctor. The
men always try to get out of it.

Medical Officer Oh, well it'll be good farming country after.

Nurse If there are any of us left to see it.

First Soldier Still got my water on the knee, doc.

Medical Officer I'll fix you up with a number nine later.

First Soldier On my knee! – I said, sir!

Sergeant All right, you men. I want this trench clear in half an hour; get stuck in. Come on, jump to it!

The **Men** *form up, as in a slit trench, digging.*

Band   OH IT'S A LOVELY WAR

(*Very slow.*)

Haig (*reading a letter*) From Snowball to Douglas. Water and mud are increasing and becoming horrible. The longer days when they come will be most welcome, especially to the officers, who say the conditions are impairing their efficiency. The other ranks don't seem to mind so much.

First Soldier Look out – we're awash! Hey, give us a hand; he's going under.

Second Soldier Cor – he's worse than old Fred.

Third Soldier Here, whatever happened to old Fred?

Second Soldier I dunno. Haven't seen him since his last cry for help.

Fourth Soldier That's right; he got sucked under.

Third Soldier Oh no, he went sick.

Fifth Soldier No, he went under.

Third Soldier He went sick.

Second Soldier He got sucked under, mate.

Third Soldier Well, I bet you a fag he went sick.

Second Soldier Don't be daft. You can't go sick here.

You've got to lose your lungs, your liver, your lights . . .

Sergeant Watch it!

The **Nurse** *crossing in front stumbles.*

First Soldier I think she's lost hers.

Nurse Thank you.

Medical Officer Put that man on a charge, sergeant.

First Soldier On a raft.

Haig Everything points to a complete breakdown in enemy morale. Now is the time to hit him resolutely and firmly. I understand the Prime Minister has been asking questions about my strategy. I cannot believe a British Minister could be so ungentlemanly.

The **Soldiers** *go off.*

Nurse (*reading back her letter to check it*) Thank you for the copy of *The Times*. I am glad that in spite of all it is still a victory; it does not seem so here. It is beyond belief, the butchery; the men look so appalling when they are brought in and so many die.

Haig September 17th. Glass still falling. A light breeze blew from the south. Weather unsettled.

Newspanel AVERAGE LIFE OF A MACHINE-GUNNER UNDER ATTACK . . . FOUR MINUTES.

The **Nurse** *goes quietly into.*

Song   KEEP THE HOME FIRES BURNING

They were summoned from the hillside,
They were called in from the glen,
And the country found them ready
At the stirring call for men.
Let no tears add to their hardship,
As the soldiers pass along,
And although your heart is breaking,
Make it sing this cheery song:

Keep the Home Fires burning
While your hearts are yearning,
Though the lads are far away,
They dream of home.
There's a silver lining,
Through the dark clouds shining,
Turn the dark cloud inside out,
Till the boys come home.

Newspanel   SEPT 20 ... MENIN ROAD ... BRITISH LOSS
22,000 MEN GAIN 800 YARDS ... SEPT 25 ... POLYGON WOOD
... BRITISH LOSS 17,000 MEN GAIN 1,000 YARDS.

During the newspanel two **Lancashire Lasses** *walk across the stage, as if walking along a street.*

First Girl   Hey look, another casualty list. (*She goes with the* **Second Girl** *to look at the list.*) Makes you shiver, don't it?

Second Girl   Ee! All those Arkwrights. That's three she's lost.

First Girl   Four. It'll be 'Arry this time, used to be a loom jobber.

A **Third Girl** *comes.*

Third Girl (*calls*)   What you looking at?

Second Girl   Casualty list.

Third Girl   Oh my God! Let's 'ave a look.

First Girl   All those Arkwrights. Y'know they're bringing 'em 'ome at night now, don't yer?

Third Girl   They're letting 'em out of the prisons an' all.

Second Girl   What for?

Third Girl   Because there's another big push coming, that's what I 'eard.

Second Girl   'Course, you work in munitions, don't yer?

Third Girl   Yeah, first to 'ear about these things.

First Girl Get a good screw too, don't yer?

Third Girl Yeah! One girl in my department knocked up three pounds las' week.

First Girl Get away!

Second Girl That's where the money is! Wouldn't like to work down there, tho' . . . all those men . . .

Third Girl Yeah! An' it can be a bit dangerous an' all! We 'ad an explosion only last week, one of the girls got blown to smithereens. No use worrying, tho', is it? You've just got to carry on.

First Girl We're on overtime.

Third Girl Oh yeah! You're on cotton, aren't yer? My sister works down there.

First Girl Well, they're on some funny stuff this week. They say it's for shrouds! Makes yer shiver, don't it?

They all shiver.

Third Girl Gives me the willies! Sooner be on munitions.

Band   WALTZING MATILDA

The music is distant at first.

Second Girl What's that then?

First Girl It's a band, innit?

They run downstage and peer out towards the back of the audience.

Third Girl It's the Aussies! (*Shouts.*) Up the Aussies!

*The **Girls** smile and wave.*

Newspanel OCT 12 . . . PASSCHENDAELE . . . BRITISH LOSS 13,000 MEN IN 3 HOURS . . . GAIN 100 YARDS.

Third Girl Don't they look brown!

First Girl 'Andsome.

Second Girl   Lovely fellers!

They all shout, 'Up the Aussies!' 'Up the Anzacs!'

First Girl   Oh, they've gone.

Band   WALTZING MATILDA FADES OUT

Third Girl   My sister goes out with an Aussie.

First Girl   What the one in shrouds?

Third Girl   No, she's on shirts. (*Half singing.*) Sister Susie's sewin' shirts for soldiers ... (*To the* **Band.**) Give us a note.

She is humming the tune.

Second Girl (*to* **First Girl**)   Come on, we'll be late for work.

First *and* **Second Girl**   Ta ra! See you later!

The **First** *and* **Second Girl** *go. The* **Third Girl** *sings.*

Song   SISTER SUSIE'S SEWING SHIRTS

Sister Susie's sewing shirts for soldiers,
Such skill at sewing shirts my shy young sister Susie
    shows,
Some soldiers send epistles, say they'd sooner sleep on
    thistles,
Than the saucy, soft, short shirts for soldiers, sister Susie
    sews.

Third Girl (*to the audience*)   Hey, the war won't go on for ever. Let's sing, shall we? If I sing it again, will you join in with me?

She sings.

Sister Susie's sewing shirts for soldiers,
Such skill at sewing shirts my shy young sister Susie
    shows,
Some soldiers send epistles, say they'd sooner sleep on
    thistles,
Than the saucy, soft, short shirts for soldiers, sister Susie
    sews.

She sings the chorus at double speed, but doesn't sing the last line, saying to the audience:

Can't 'ear you! etc. (*When the song finishes.*) I'm off to work now. Ta ta.

Two **Pierrots** *come on with three hats.*

Newspanel   800,000 GERMANS STARVE TO DEATH THROUGH BRITISH BLOCKADE.

First Pierrot (*wearing British General's hat*)   The prospects for 1918 are excellent. This year will see final victory.

Second Pierrot (*wearing German helmet*)   Sieg für Deutschland.

First Pierrot (*putting on French kepi*)   Et pour la France la gloire et la victoire.

Second Pierrot (*wearing German helmet*)   Gott mit uns. (*Puts on British General's hat.*) And with us, old boy. If we continue this campaign the way we are going, we'll sew the entire thing up by 1918.

First Pierrot (*putting on German helmet*)   Neunzehn hundert, neunzehn.

Second Pierrot   Nineteen, twenty, twenty-five.

First Pierrot   Fünf und zwanzig, dreissig . . .

Second Pierrot   Thirty, thirty-five . . . forty, forty-five, fifty, fifty-five, sixty, sixty-three, sixty-four – any advance on sixty-four? Plenty more numbers where they came from.

The three **Lancashire Lasses** *reappear.*

The **Pierrots** *and the* **Girls**   Some soldiers send epistles, say they'd sooner sleep on thistles,
    Than the saucy, soft, short shirts for soldiers,
    Sister Susie sews.

Exeunt.

Band   MARSEILLAISE

French Soldiers *line up for an advance.*

French Officer Alors. Again for the glory of France, prepare for the attack. En avant! . . . En avant! . . . Are you deaf?

French Soldier Non, mon capitaine.

French Officer What is this? A mutiny?

French Soldier We think it is stupid to go into the trenches again.

French Officer You don't think – you obey. If you refuse, you will be shot!

French Soldier Very well. We follow you – like lambs to the slaughter.

French Officer Bon. Like lambs to the slaughter . . . Pour la gloire de la France! En avant!

French Soldier Baaa.

French Officer Vive la République!

The **Men** *begin to advance towards the footlights.*

Soldiers Baaa.

French Officer En avant!

Soldiers Baaa – baa.

French Officer *and* **Soldiers** Baaa – baaa – baaa . . .

There is a burst of machine-gun fire. They collapse. Pause.

French Soldier Adieu la vie.

In believable French accents, all sing.

Song   CHANSON DE CRAONNE

> Adieu la vie,
> Adieu l'amour,
> Adieu à toutes les femmes.
> C'est bien fini,
> C'est pour toujours,

De cette guerre infâme.
C'est à Craonne,
Sur le plateau,
Qu'ils ont laissé leur peau:
Car ils sont tous condamnés,
Ce sont les sacrifiés.

Song   I DON'T WANT TO BE A SOLDIER

I don't want to be a soldier,
I don't want to go to war,
I'd rather stay at home,
Around the streets to roam,
And live off the earnings of a lady typist.

Newspanel THE WAR TO END WARS ... KILLED TEN
MILLION ... WOUNDED TWENTY-ONE MILLION ... MISSING
SEVEN MILLION.

I don't want a bayonet in my belly,
I don't want my bollocks shot away,
I'd rather stay in England,
In merry, merry England,
And fornicate my bleeding life away.

Slide Sequence:
Slide 42: Repeated.
*Slide 48: Canadian infantrymen in trench. One fast asleep, another
   writing home.*
Slide 31: Repeated.
Slide 49: Five Tommies trying to pull a field gun out of the mud.
*Slide 50: A company of French Poilus marching past with rifles at
   the slope.*
*Slide 51: Two weary British officers, both in battle dress, one with
   bandaged head.*
*Slide 52: Two young Canadian soldiers, leaning against spiked
   boards, one writing a letter.*
*Slide 53: A long line of Tommies walking away from the camera,
   following the direction of a trench.*

Song   AND WHEN THEY ASK US

(*Tune: 'They wouldn't believe me'*)

The **Men** *sing.*

[42] And when they ask us, how dangerous it was, [48]
Oh, we'll never tell them, no, we'll never tell them: [31]
We spent our pay in some café, [49]
And fought wild women night and day,
'Twas the cushiest job we ever had. [50]

And when they ask us, and they're certainly going to ask
   us, [51]
The reason why we didn't win the Croix de Guerre, [52]
Oh, we'll never tell them, oh, we'll never tell them [53]
There was a front, but damned if we knew where.

Finale   OH IT'S A LOVELY WAR

The **Women** *join in.*

Oh, oh, oh, it's a lovely war,
What do we want with eggs and ham,
When we've got plum and apple jam?
Form fours, right turn,
How shall we spend the money we earn?
Oh, oh, oh, it's a lovely,
Oh, oh, oh, it's a lovely,
Oh, oh, oh, it's a lovely war!

CURTAIN

Afterword

by Victor Spinetti

I didn't relish the idea of a show about World War One. The thought of that war made me sick. Poppy day, the Last Post, silence at the Cenotaph! All those young lives lost! To what purpose? God, how I hated those songs! But Gerry Raffles assured us it was only the way the BBC crowd sang them. Joan said she agreed and began to distribute books, memoirs and histories by men who'd lived through it all, poets and patricians, generals and general dogsbodies. There were copies of *The Illustrated War News*, which was published during that war, photographs, statistics and paper for notes.

We all knew something of the background to that war but I never knew that all the fuses for the shells were made in Britain and that the Germans bought their share from us, during the war. I didn't know that the women who worked in the munitions factories had their hands dyed yellow, permanently, from the saltpetre. Nor did I have any idea of our losses in that war. Ten million dead. Twenty-one million wounded. Seven million missing. At Passchendaele alone, thirteen thousand men were lost in three hours. Haig's comment was, 'Mostly gamekeepers and servants'.

They'd gained one hundred yards.

Joan had a way of working of her own. One of the earliest sessions stays in my mind. It was a trench scene.

'Put out all the lights in the theatre,' she said, 'Rehearsal lighting, exit signs too.'

The men on stage were sitting or half lying down. It was very dark. Only a little grey light filtered in high up in the flies.

'Half of you make your way to the back of the stalls. Not a sound, mind. Right? Now listen . . .'

Long silence . . .

Someone at the back changed position and clutched at a seat.

'What was that?' she asked the group on stage. Several guessed. One got it right.

'Who was it?' No one knew. 'Listen again. . . . What can you hear outside?'

We told her, one by one. Someone actually heard the traffic on Stratford Broadway, a quarter of a mile away.

'Well that's how it would be when one says, "They're copping it down Railway Wood tonight."'

'That's Hill sixty.'

'No, not that. . . . Listen! . . .'

And she made Colin Kemball climb the highest ladder to the flies to sing, 'Stille Nacht'.

'It's somebody singing.'

'Is it those Welsh bastards in the next trench?'

'No, it's Jerry!'

They kept that atmosphere, throughout the run.

There was a drill scene in Joan's outline and Gerry contacted a real army sergeant and asked him to drill us.

'We'll get this right, if nothing else,' said Gerry.

Well, the sergeant arrived just when we were working on the gentle promenade scene.

'Clear the decks!' he commanded, 'And no women!'

The women disappeared. I didn't know but they crept quietly into the gallery, to enjoy the fun.

'Where are your rifles?'

'We don't have any . . . sir.' said Murray Melvin.

'That's O.K. The Old Contemptibles didn't 'ave none neither, when war broke out.'

'Will these do?' said Murray. He'd found some walking sticks and a sunshade from the promenade scene. With a lot of bullying and blaspheming the drill sergeant took over. It may have done us all good but it was far too obscene for public consumption, let alone the Lord Chamberlain.

'What can we do with it?' said Joan, 'I don't want to lose his expression.'

'Don't think the audience would have a clue as to what he was saying.' I told her, 'I know I didn't when I was in the army. It was "Yer uckenspinskerdereye. Yersilbucharficsuden."'

'That's it!' she cried, 'You've got it! Do it in gibberish! Try it!'

I went right into it. The men played up. When I turned around Joan was crying with laughter.

'They'd give a thousand quid for that at the Palladium.'

Indeed, that's how I remember working with her, gales of laughter. She could get mad and throw her hat at us but the next minute she'd be laughing.

'I've just committed a murder!' she said one day, after she'd thrown out some inquisitive journalist. Then she burst out laughing.

Joan was my university. We were never without books – books about architecture, art, music, literature, language, poetry. We'd delve into the backgrounds of the plays we did, and of some we couldn't afford to do. There would be great discussions sometimes. The most timid person would suddenly prove to be the cleverest.

Joan should have been running an academy of Dramatic Art. If you wanted to understand her, you'd have to pull back the camera, first, finding her in the part of London the theatre was in, then in the city and then this island, finally, the world.

She spoiled me for much of the West End acting. Often, when I go to the theatre, I feel like shouting, 'No! I don't believe you!' Not because they're wrong but because they're all doing it so beautifully.

So, it seems, If you're to act truly, you must stop 'acting'. It sounds ridiculous but it only means cutting the superfluous, cutting trying to be great . . .

Alright, so you're feeling depressed tonight. Well, be depressed. Hamlet or Falstaff or whoever it is, will soon recover their spirits. Even if you're in mourning . . . Well, who isn't? Just don't try forcing yourself to be full of joy. Don't rise to a performance. Just step on to that stage. You've come from the place you've discovered. Now, you're there!

Our work at Stratford was not interpretation. It was creation. You don't invent a character. You imagined everything that surrounded him, influenced him, gave him his history.

We never learnt a line. We were never given moves. We knew, instinctively, where we would be in relation to the other characters. On a two-minute scene, in which you weren't playing a leading part but just walking the street, hearing a shot – learning that Archduke Ferdinand had been assassinated – she might spend hours. We had to re-evaluate everything, question God, religion, the state, power, belief and disbelief.

'Here's your cybernetics,' she told us, 'Put all your findings into a computer, with your loves, hates and fears – don't leave them out, they're your strength . . . And then, forget them all. You don't worry about such things when you're on stage.'

On our opening night, in Stratford, I was standing in the wings when the glow of a cigarette appeared. It was herself.

'We don't have an opening for the show.' she said.

'Yes, you do! You have "Row, Row, Row".'

'That's a song, not an opening. Why don't you go out there and talk to the audience?'

'Me? What about?'

'Don't ask me! You always have plenty to say for yourself. Ask them how they are – and wait for an answer – but don't tell jokes!'

Well, I did it! For the first time in my life I just stood there and talked to friends. Joan wanted me to break the ice, to destroy the barrier between them and us. Perhaps she thought it would encourage them to participate in the show. The proscenium arch has often served as a rood screen behind which the priests perform their mystery and magic. It can be of service, of course, if you wish to distance your picture by framing it. In our case, we needed them with us for our lovely war.

So, every night I would go out and talk, sometimes for a minute, sometimes for a while. If anyone joined in, as they did at Stratford, it became a feature of the show. Sometimes I felt like the chap running the Pierrot troupe – on the beach at Ramsgate.

'Everybody in? Only twenty of you? We'd better get going. If it comes on to rain, we'll get the deck chairs wet.'

One night, a journalist from one of the big papers was supposed to be coming. We went up on time. There was no sign of him. We carried on as usual. It must have been close on ten minutes before he rolled up.

'Hullo!' I shouted, 'Good evening. Where have you been?'

He was embarrassed.

'Couldn't find a parking space.' he muttered.

'You've missed some of my best bits. We could go back and do it again.'

'No!' from some of the audience. And we went on.

Lovely War was one of the two shows I was proud to be in. The other was *The Hostage* by Brendan Behan, where we let fall all the world's flags when we heard that the young hostage, who'd been parked with us, was about to be shot. But *Lovely War* wasn't just a show. It was a revelation.

Appendix

Source material for 'OH WHAT A LOVELY WAR'

'The Times' History of the War
'I Was There', published weekly about 1934, later assembled into three volumes and published by Amalgamated Press
The First World War, Colonel Repington (2 volumes)
My War Memories, General Ludendorff (2 volumes)
Earl Haig, Brigadier-General Charteris
Haig, Duff Cooper
Haig's Diaries
Field-Marshal Wilson, Sir C. E. Callwell
War Memoirs, Lloyd George
How We Lived Then – 1914–1918, Mrs C. S. Peel
C.Q.G., Jean Pierrefeu
Mutiny 1917, John Williams
Memoirs of an Infantry Officer, Siegfried Sassoon
Undertones of War, Edmund Blunden
In Flanders Fields, Leon Wolff
Mr Punch's History of the War
A History of the World War, Liddell Hart
The First World War, Cyril Falls
Memoirs, Franz von Papen
Diplomatic Documents, H.M.S.O., 1915
1914, F. M. French
The March on Paris, 1914, General von Cluck
The First Hundred Thousand, Ian Hay
Regimental Histories
The Great War, H. W. Wilson (13 volumes)
August 1914, B. Tuchman
Brass Hat: The Story of General Wilson
The Donkeys, Alan Clark
The Illustrated War News (published weekly during the war)
Contemporary newspapers (in the possession of G. Sewell)
European History 1815–1918, C. J. Pennithorne Hughes
Pageant of the Century, Odhams Press, published 1935

Covenants with Death, Express Newspapers
The First World War, Illustrated Express Newspapers
World War, published weekly about 1937
Twenty Years After, published weekly 1937
The Great War (The World Crisis), Winston Churchill
A Soldier's Diary, Ralph Scott
Memoirs of a Foxhunting Man, Siegfried Sassoon
Goodbye to All That, Robert Graves
The '*Phillip Maddison*' series of novels by Henry Williamson
Mons, John Terraine
Official History of the War
Die Blutige International, Kirsch
Works of Phillip Noel-Baker
Merchants of Death, Engelbrecht and Hanighen
Works of Herman Kahn
Verdun, Jules Romains
Covenant with Death, John Harris
The Sphere, Illustrated London News
Writings of Philip Gibbs
Records of: *The Times, Daily Express, Daily Mail, Evening Standard*
Charles Chilton's notes and songs, and many other publications
of which no note has been kept.

Music and Visual Aids

For information on where to obtain slides, news panel, song
books and musical scores etc., apply to: (*in U.K.*) *Samuel French, 52
Fitzroy Street, London W1P 6JR;* (*in U.S.A. and Canada*) Amy E. Love,
Wedgewood Productions, P.O. Box 440, Crownsville, MD
21032, and/or 600 Cornelius Point Rd, Stevensville, MD 21666
USA.

For a complete catalogue of Methuen Drama titles
write to:

Methuen Drama
Bloomsbury Publishing Plc
50 Bedford Square
London WC1B 3DP

or you can visit our website at:

www.bloomsbury.com